NECRONOMICON
EX MORTIS

By HR Giger

Introduction

A lot of ink actual and virtual spilled on the subject of the Necronomicon. Some have derided it as a clumsy hoax; others have praised it as a powerful grimoire. As the decades have passed, more information has come to light both on the book's origins and discovery, and on the information contained within its pages. The Necronomicon has been found to contain formula for spiritual transformation, consistent with some of the most ancient mystical processes in the world, processes that involve communion with the stars.

Table of Contents

SUPPLEMENTARY MATERIAL
TO 777

THE CHART that follows is based on research presently available to the Editor with regard to Sumerian and Assyro-Babylonian religions. Entries in parentheses refer to the state of correspondences before the advent of the Elder Gods, the Race of MARDUK; that is, it reflects the nature of the cosmos before the Fall of MARDUK from Heaven. (Names of zodiacal constellations are after Budge's renderings.)

	Table VII [A.C.]	Table XXV [S.]	
0.	...	ANU (TIAMAT)	
1.	Sphere of the Primum Mobile	ENLIL (ABSU)	
2.	Sphere of the Zodiac or Fixed Stars	ENKI; LUMASHI (IGIGI)	
3.	Sphere of Saturn	ADAR	
4.	Sphere of Jupiter	MARDUK	
5.	Sphere of Mars	NERGAL	
6.	Sphere of the Sun	UTU	
7.	Sphere of Venus	INANNA	
8.	Sphere of Mercury	NEBO	
9.	Sphere of the Moon	NANNA	
10.	Sphere of the Elements	KIA	
11.	Air	ANNA	
12.	Mercury	GUDUD	
13.	Moon	SIN	
14.	Venus	DLIBAT	
1	Aries	AGRU (XUBUR)	

5.			
1 6.	Taurus	KAKKAB U ALAP SHAME (KINGU)	
1 7.	Gemini	RE'U KINU SHAME U TU'AME RABUTI	
		(VIPER)	
1 8.	Cancer	SHITTU (SNAKE)	
1 9.	Leo	KALBU RABU (LAKHAMU)	
2 0.	Virgo	SHIRU (WHIRLWIND)	
2 1.	Jupiter	UMUNPADDU	

22.	Libra	ZIBANITUM (Ravening Dog)
23.	Water	BADUR
24.	Scorpio	AKRABU (SCORPION-MAN)
25.	Sagittarius	PA-BIL-SAG (HURRICANE)
26.	Capricorn	SUXUR MASH (FISH-MAN)
27.	Mars	MASTABARRU
28.	Aquarius	GULA (HORNED BEAST)
29.	Pisces	DILGAN U RIKIS NUNI (WEAPON)
30.	Sun	SHAMASH
30.	Fire	AG
30.	Saturn	KAIMANU
30.	(bis) Earth	KIA
30.	(bis) Spirit	ZI

NOTES ON PRONUNCIATION

WE CANNOT BE absolutely how Sumerian and Akkadian were spoken; but many useful guidelines are available to the student, including the transliterated tablets found all over Mesopotamia. Basically, we can offer the following principles which should prove of value in reciting the foreign language instructions :

Vowels

a

as in "f*a*ther"

e

as in "wh*ey*"

i

as in "ant*i*que"

o

as in "b*oa*t" (but rarely found)

u

as in "z*u*lu"

Consonants

Most are basically the same as in English. The Sumerians did not have an alphabet as we know it, but they had developed a syllabary, very much like the Japanese "Kana" script of today. In phonetic transliterations, the English spelling sought to approximate the Sumerian pronunciation. However, there are a few sounds which English does not possess, and which have been put into phonetic variations. Important examples below :

X

as in the German "ach"

CH

(same as above)

Q

as in "like"

K

(same as above)

SH

as in "shall"

SS

as in, perhaps, "lasso"; a hissing "s" common to Arabic languages

Z

as in "lots"; a hard "ts" sound, not quite as in "zoo"

Remember, in the transliterations which follow, every letter must be pronounced. There are no schwas or silent syllables in Sumerian. Hence, "KIA" is pronounced "keeya"; "KAIMANU" is pronounced "ka-ee-mah-nu" or, if spoken rapidly, the two initial vowel sounds slur into 'kigh' rhyming with "high"

The incantations should be said carefully and slowly at first, to familiarise oneself with the tongue-twisting phrases. A mistake may prove fatal to the Work

THE SPELLS (TRANSLATED)

WHERE POSSIBLE, the Editor has taken every opportunity to find the original Sumerian or Akkadian translation of a given Greek charm of conjuration. These will be given here. Also, the reader will find English translations of the Sumerian charms as they are given in the NECRONOMICON. Not al of the charms are available this way, and sometimes we have had to make do with near misses. Much of what is found here has

come from the Maklu text, of which the only extant translation is in the German of Tallqvist ("Die Assyrische Beschworungsserie Maqlu nach dem originalen im British Museum Herausgegeben" Acta Societatis Scientiarum Fennicae, Tomm. XX, No. 6, Helsingforsiae mdcccxcv). The word "maklu" or "maqlu" itself is controversial, but Tallqvist seems to think that it does, indeed, mean "burning"; especially so as the incantations to be found therein invariably entail burning something, usually a doll made in the likeness of a witch or evil sorcerer that the magician wished to dispose of. Hence, we have here probably the archetype of the Great Burning Times of the Inquisition, when people were condemned to a fiery death as Witches and Pagans. The chant "burn, witch! burn!" can be found in the Maklu text, in all its pristine glory. Indeed, Cthulhu Calls.

The Conjuration "The Binding of the Evil Sorcerers"

Alsi ku nushi ilani mushiti

Itti kunu alsi mushitum kallatum kuttumtum
Alsi bararitum qablitum u namaritum
Ashshu kashshaptu u kashshipanni
Eli nitum ubbiraanni
Ili-ia u Ishtari-ia ushis-su-u-eli -ia
Eli ameri-ia amru-usanaku
Imdikula salalu musha u urra Qu-
u imtana-allu-u pi-ia
Upu unti pi-ia iprusu
Me mashtiti -ia umattu-u
Eli li nubu-u xiduti si-ipdi

Izizanimma ilani rabuti shima-a dababi
Dini dina alakti limda
Epu-ush salam kashshapi-ia u kashshapti-ia
Sha epishia u mushtepishti-ia
Is mass-ssarati sha mushi lipshuru ruxisha limnuti
Pisha lu-u ZAL.LU Lishanusha Lu-u Tabtu
Sha iqbu-u amat limutti-ia kima ZAL.LU litta-tuk
Sha ipushu kishpi kima Tabti lishxarmit qi-
ishrusha pu-uttu-ru ipshetusha xulluqu
Kal amatusha malla-a sseri Ina
qibit iqbu-u ilani mushitum.

The Conjuration "XILQA XILQA BESA BESA" or "A Most Excellent Charm
Against the Hordes of Demons" etc.

Arise! Arise! Go far away! Go far away!

Be shamed! Be shamed! Flee! Flee!
Turn around, go, arise and go far away!

Your wickedness may rise to heaven like unto smoke! Arise and leave my body!

From my body, depart in shame! From my body flee!

Turn away from my body! Go away from my body! Do not
return to my body! Do no come near my body! Do not
approach my body!

Do not throng around my body!
Be commanded by Shammash the Mighty! Be commanded by Enki, Lord of
All!

Be commanded by Marduk, the Great Magician of the Gods! Be commanded by the God of Fire, your Destroyer!

May you be held back from my body!

"Another Binding of the Sorcerers"

Ssalmani-ia ana pagri tapqida duppira

Ssalmani-ia ana pagri taxira duppira
Ssalmani-ia iti pagri tushni-illa duppira
Ssalmani ini ishdi pagri tushni-illa duppira
Ssalmani-ia qimax pagri taqbira duppira
Ssalmani-ia ana qulqullati tapqida duppira

Ssalmani-ia ina igari tapxa-a duppira
Ssalmani-ia ina askuppati Tushni-illa duppira
Ssalmani-ia ina bi'sha duri tapxa-a duppira
Ssalmani-ia ana GISHBAR tapqida duppira

The Conjuration of the Mountains of MASHU"

May the mountain overpower you!

May the mountain hold you back!
May the mountain conquer you!
May the mountain frighten you!
May the mountain shake you to the core!
May the mountain hold you in check!
May the mountain subject you!
May the mountain cover you!
May the mighty mountain fall on you,
May you be held back from my body!

(Note: the original translator had noted the resemblance between the Greek word for Lors, kurios, and the Sumerian word for mountain, kur, and for a type of underworld, chthoic, monster which is also called kur and which refers to the Leviathan of the Old Testament.

Also, in this particular conjuration, the word for mountain is shadu - shaddai ? The Old Serpent KUR is, of course, invoked every day by the Christians: Kyrie Eleison!)

COMMON SUMERIAN WORDS AND PHRASES IN ENGLISH

	Sumerian	English	
	Akhkharu	Vampire	
	Alal	Destroyer	
	Alla Xul	Evil God	
	Barra!	Begone!	
	Dingir Xul	Evil God	
	Edin Na Zu!	Go to the Desert! (a form of exorcism)	
	Gelal	Incubus	
	Gigim xul	Evil Spirit	
	Gidim Xul	Evil Ghost	
	Idimmu	Demon	
	Idpa	Fever	
	Kashshaptu	Witch	
	Lalartu	Phantom	
	Lalssu	Spectre	
	Lilit	Succubus	
	Maskim Xul	Evil Fiend (Ambusher, Lier-In-Wait)	
	Mulla Xul	Evil Devil	
	Rabishu	(same as Maskim Xul)	
	Telal	Wicked Demon (Warrior)	
	Uggae	God of Death	
	Uruku	Larvae	
	Utuk Xul	Evil Spirit	

Zi Dingir Anna Kanpa! Spirit, God of the Sky, Remember!

Zi Dinger Kia Kanpa! Spirit, God of the Earth, Remember!

A WORD CONCERNING THE ORIGINAL

MANUSCRIPT

THE EDITOR and the Publishers anticipate that there will be a demand at first for privileged views of the original NECRONOMICON, whether out of curiosity's sake, or by nervous experimenters who will be certain that we did not copy a sigil correctly, etc. Let us hasten to state at this point that the original Ms. is neither the property of the Editor, nor the Publishers. We were given the right to translate and publish this work, with as much additional and explanatory material as needed, but not the right to hold the MS. up to public inspection. We regret that this is the case, but we also feel that it might be advisable, in reference to the dangerous character of the work involved. Perhaps one day a book will be written on the hazards of possessing such an original work in one's home or office, including the fearful hallucinations, physical incapacities, and emotional malaise that accompanied this work from the onset of the translation to the end of its final published form.

Therefore, as a matter of policy, we cannot honour any requests to see the NECRONOMICON in its original state.

BANISHINGS

Read this section carefully.

In the interim period between the translation and the publication of this work, the Editor, along with a circle of initiates in another discipline, undertook to experiment with the rituals and forces outlined in the NECRONOMICON. In using the material alone, or within a Western ceremonial structure (such as the Golden Dawn system) we came upon startling discoveries in both cases: there are no effective banishings for the forces invoked in the NECRONOMICON itself! The rituals, incantations, formulae of this Book are of ancient origin, comprising some of the oldest written magickal workings in

Western occult history. the deities and demons identified within have probably not been effectively summoned in nearly six thousand years. Ordinary exorcisms and banishing formulae have thus far proved extremely inadequate: this, by experienced magicians. Hence, the following recommendations.

The religion of the ancient Sumerian peoples seems to have been lunar-oriented, a religion - or religion - magickal structure - of the night, of darkness in a sense. Invocations using solar formulae have proved thus far effective in successfully banishing NECRONOMICON demons and intelligences. For instance, the Kaddish prayer of the Jewish faith contains some solar elements that have proved resilient to inimical genii, and the vibration of the Lord's Prayer for Christians is also a workable method.

We suggest that individual operators utilise an equivalent solar (i.e., positive light) invocation from their own religion or the religion of their ancestors, should the no longer have a religion or should they have changed it in their lifetime.

For best practical purposes in the beginning - for those intent on actually using the rituals contained herein - it is advisable to take especial care in the construction of the magickal circle and of all magickal defences. A preliminary period of purification is well in order before attempting anything in this grimoire. Persons of unstable mental condition, or unstable emotional condition, should not be allowed, under any circumstances, to observe one of these rituals in progress. That would be criminal, and perhaps in suicidal. One of our colleagues was fearfully attacked by his dog directly following a fairly simple and uncomplicated formula from this book. This is definitely not a Gilbert chemistry set.

The method of the NECRONOMICON concerns deep, primeval forces that seem to pre-exist the normal archetypal images of the tarot trumps and the Golden Dawn telesmatic figures. These are forces that developed outside the Judeo-Christian mainstream, and were worshipped and summoned long before the creation of the Qabala as we know it today. Hence, the ineffectiveness of the Golden Dawn banishing procedures against them. They are not necessarily demonic or qliphotic in the sense that these terms are commonly understood in the West, they just simply represent power sources largely untapped and thus far ignored by twentieth-century, mainstream consciousness.

The results of any experimentation with this book, as well as practical suggestions concerning its rituals, are welcomed by the publishers.

THE TESTIMONY OF THE MAD ARAB

THIS is the testimony of all that I have seen, and all that I have learned, in those years that I have possessed the Three Seals of MASSHU. I have seen One Thousand-and-One moons, and surely this is enough for the span of a man's life, though it is said the Prophets lived much longer. I am weak, and ill, and bear a great tiredness and exhaustion, and a sigh hangs in my breast like a dark lantern. I am old.

The wolves carry my name in their midnight speeches, and that quiet, subtle Voice is summoning me from afar. And a Voice much closer will shout into my ear with unholy impatience. The weight of my soul will decide its final resting place. Before that time, I

must put down here all that I can concerning the horrors that stalk Without, and which lie in wait at the door of every man, for this is the ancient arcana that has been handed down of old, but which has been forgotten by all but a few men, the worshippers of the Ancient Ones (may their names be blotted out!).

And if I do not finish this task, take what is here and discover the rest, for time is short and mankind does not know nor understand the evil that awaits it, from every side, from every Gate, from every broken barrier, from every mindless acolyte at the alters of madness.

For this is the Book of the Dead, the Book of the Black Earth, that I have writ down at the peril of my life, exactly as I received it, on the planes of the IGIGI, the cruel celestial spirits from beyond the Wanderers of the Wastes.

Let all who read this book be warned thereby that the habitation of men are seen and surveyed by that Ancient Race of gods and demons from a time before time, and that they seek revenge for that forgotten battle that took place somewhere in the Cosmos and rent the Worlds in the days before the creation of Man, when the Elder Gods walked the

Spaces, the race of MARDUK, as he is known to the Chaldeans, and of ENKI our MASTER, the Lord of Magicians.

Know, then, that I have trod all the Zones of the Gods, and also the places of the Azonei, and have descended unto the foul places of Death and Eternal Thirst, which may be reached through the Gate of GANZIR, which was built in UR, in the days before Babylon was.

Know, too, that I have spoken with all manner of spirit and daemon, whose names are no longer known in the societies of Man, or were never known. And the seals of some of these are writ herein; yet others I must take with me when I leave you. ANU have mercy on my soul!

I have seen the Unknown Lands, that no map has ever charted. I have lived in the deserts and the wastelands, and spoken with demons and the souls of slaughtered men, and of women who have dies in childbirth, victims of the she-fiend LAMMASHTA.

I have traveled beneath the Seas, in search of the Palace of Our Master, and found the stone of monuments of vanquished civilisations, and deciphered the writings of some of these; while still others remain mysteries to any man who lives. And these civilisations were destroyed because of the knowledge contained in this book.

I have traveled among the stars, and trembled before the Gods. I have, at last, found the formulae by which I passed the Gate ARZIR, and passed into the forbidden realms of the foul IGIGI.

I have raised demons, and the dead.

I have summoned the ghosts of my ancestors to real and visible appearance on the tops of temples built to reach the stars, and built to touch the nethermost cavities of HADES. I have wrestled with the Black Magician, AZAG-THOTH, in vain, and fled to the Earth by calling upon INANNA and her brother MARDUK, Lord of the double-headed AXE.

I have raised armies against the Lands of the East, by summoning the hordes of fiends I have made subject unto me, and so doing found NGAA, the God of the heathens, who breathes flame and roars like a thousand thunders.

I have found fear.

I have found the Gate that leads to the Outside, by which the Ancient Ones, who ever seek entrance to our world, keep eternal watch. I have smelled the vapours of that Ancient One, Queen of the Outside, whose name is writ in the terrible MAGAN text, the testament of some dead civilisation whose priests, seeking power, swing open the dread, evil Gate for an hour past the time, and were consumed.

I came to possess this knowledge through circumstances quite peculiar, while still the unlettered son of a shepherd in what is called Mesopotamia by the Greeks.

When I was only a youth, travelling alone in the mountains to the East, called MASSHU by the people who live there, I came upon a grey rock carved with three strange symbols. It stood as high as a man, and as wide around as a bull. It was firmly in the ground, and I could not move it. Thinking no more of the carvings, save that they might be the work of a king to mark some ancient victory over an enemy, I built a fire at its foot to protect me from the wolves that wander in those regions and went to sleep, for it was night and I was far from my village, being Bet Durrabia. Being about three hours from dawn, in the nineteenth of Shabatu, I was awakened by the howl of a dog, perhaps of a wolf, uncommonly loud and close at hand. The fire had dies to its embers, and these red, glowing coals cast a faint, dancing shadow across the stone monument with the three carvings. I began to make haste to build another fire when, at once, the gray rock began to rise slowly into the air, as though it were a dove. I could not move or speak for the fear that seized upon my spine and wrapped cold fingers around my skull. The Dik of Azug-bel-ya was no stranger to me than this sight, though the former seemed to melt into my hands!

Presently, I heard a voice, softly, some distance away and a more practical fear, that of the possibility of robbers, took hold of me and I rolled behind some weeds, trembling. Another voice joined the first, and soon several men in the black robes of thieves came together over the place where I was, surrounding the floating rock, of which they did not exhibit the least fright.

I could see clearly now that the three carvings on the stone monument were glowing a flame red colour, as though the rock were on fire. The figures were murmuring together in prayer or invocation, of which only a few words could be heard, and these in some unknown tongue; though, ANU have mercy on my soul!, these rituals are not unknown to

me any longer.

The figures, whose faces I could not see or recognise, began to make wild passes in the air with knives that glinted cold and sharp in the mountain night.

From beneath the floating rock, out of the very ground where it had sat, came rising the tail of a serpent. This serpent was surely larger than any I had ever seen. The thinnest section thereof was fully that of the arms of two men, and as it rose from the earth it was followed by another, although the end of the first was not seen as it seemed to reach down into the very Pit itself. These were followed by still more, and the ground began to tremble under the pressure of so many of these enormous arms. The chanting of the priests, for I knew them now to be the servants of some hidden Power, became much louder and very nearly hysterical.

IA! IA! ZI AZAG!

IA! IA!! ZI AZKAK!
IA! IA! KUTULU ZI KUR!
IA!

The ground where I was hiding became wet with some substance, being slightly downhill from the scene I was witnessing. I touched the wetness and found it to be blood. In horror, I screamed and gave my presence away to the priests. They turned toward me, and I saw a loathing that they had cut their chests with the daggers they had used to raise the stone, for some mystical purpose I could not then divine; although I know now that blood is the very food of these spirits, which is why the field after the battles of war glows with an unnatural light, the manifestations of the spirits feeding thereon.

May ANU protect us all!

My scream had the effect of casting their ritual into chaos and disorder. I raced through the mountain path by which I had come, and the priests came running after me, although some seemed to stay behind, perhaps to finish the Rites. However, as I ran wildly down the slopes in the cold night, my heart giving rise in my chest and my head growing hot, the sound of splitting rocks and thunder came from behind me and shook the very ground I ran upon. In fright, and in haste, I fell to the earth.

Rising, I turned to face whatever attacker had come nearest me, though I was unarmed. To my surprise what I saw was no priest of ancient horror, no necromancer of that forbidden Art, but black robes fallen upon the grass and weeds, with no seeming presence of life or bodies beneath them.

I walked cautiously to the first and, picking up a long twig, lifted the robe from the tangle of weeds and thorns. All that remained of the priest was a pool of slime, like green oil, and the smell of a body lain long to rot in the sun. Such a stench nearly overpowered me, but I was resolute to find the others, to see if the same fortune had also befallen them.

Walking back up the slope that I had so fearfully run down only moments ago, I came across yet another of the dark priests, in identical condition to the first. I kept walking, passing more of the robes as I went, not venturing to overturn them any longer. Then, I finally came upon the grey stone monument that had risen unnaturally into the air at the command of the priests. It now upon the ground once more, but the carvings still glowed with supernatural light. The serpents, or what I had then though of as serpents, had disappeared. But in the dead embers of the fire, now cold and black, was a shining metal plate. I picked it up and saw that it also was carved, as the stone, but very intricately, after a fashion I could not understand. I did not bear the same markings as the stone, but I had the feeling I could almost read the characters, but could not, as though I once knew the tongue but had since long forgotten. My head began to ache as though a devil was pounding my skull, when a shaft of moonlight struck the metal amulet, for I know now what it was, and a voice entered into my head and told me the secrets of the scene I had witnessed in one word:

KUTULU.

In that moment, as though whispered fiercely into my ear, I understood.

These are the signs carved upon the grey stone, that was the Gate to the Outside:

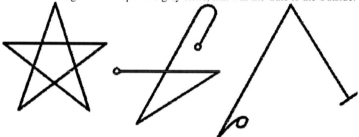

An this is the amulet that I held in my hand, and hold to this very day, around my neck as I write these words:

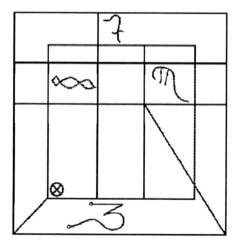

Of the three carved symbols, the first is the sign of our Race from beyond the Stars, and is called ARRA in the tongue of the Scribe who taught it to me, an emissary of the Elder Ones. In the tongue of the eldest city of Babylon, it was UR. It is the Sigil of the Covenant of the Elder Gods, and when they see it, they who gave it to us, they will not forget us. They have sworn!

Spirit of the Skies, Remember!

The second is the Elder Sign, and is the Key whereby the Powers of the Elder Gods may be summoned, when used with the proper words and shapes. It has a Name, and is called AGGA.

The third sign is the Sigil of the Watcher. It is called BANDAR. The Watcher is a Race sent by the Elder Ones. It keeps vigil while one sleeps, provided the appropriate ritual and sacrifice has been performed,: else, if called, it will turn upon you.

These seals, to be effective, must be graven on stone and set in the ground. Or, set upon the altar of offerings. Or, carried to the Rock of Invocations. Or, engraved on the metal of one's God or Goddess, and hung about the neck, but hidden from the view of the profane. Of the three, the ARRA and the AGGA may be used separately, that is to say, singly and alone. The BANDAR, however, must never be used alone, but with one or both of the others, for the Watcher must needs be reminded of the Covenant it has sworn with the Elder Gods and our Race, else it will turn upon thee and slay thee and ravage thy town until succour is to be had from the Elder Gods by the tears of thy people and the wailing of thy women.

KAKAMMU!

The metal amulet that I retrieved from the ashes of the fire, and which caught the light of the moon, is a potent seal against whatever may come in the Gate from the Outside for, seeing it, they will retreat from thee

SAVE ONLY IF IT CATCH THE LIGHT OF THE MOON UPON ITS SURFACE

for, in the dark days of the moon, or in cloud, there can be little protection against the fiends from the Ancient Lands should they break the barrier, or be let in by their servants upon the face of the earth. In such a case, no recourse is to be had until the light of the moon shines upon the earth, for the moon is the eldest among the Zonei, and is the starry symbol of our Pact. NANNA, Father of the Gods, Remember!

Wherefore, the amulet must be engraved upon pure silver in the full light of the moon, that the moon shine upon it at its working, and the essence of the moon incantations must be performed, and the prescribed rituals as given forth in this Book. And the amulet must never be exposed to the light of the Sun, for SHAMMASH called UDU, in his jealousy, will rob the seal of its power. In such a case, it must be bathed in water of camphor, and the incantations and ritual performed once again. But, verily, it were better to engrave another.

These secrets I give to thee at the pain of my life, never to be revealed to the profane, or the banished, or the worshippers of the Ancient Serpent, but to keep within thine own heart, always silent upon these things.

Peace be to thee!

Henceforth, from that fateful night in the Mountains of MASSHU, I wandered about the country-side in search of the key to the secret knowledge that had been given me. And it was a painful and lonely journey, during which time I took no wife, called no house or village my home, and dwelt in various countries, often in caves or in the deserts, learning several tongues as a traveller might learn them, to bargain with the tradespeople and learn of their news and customs. But my bargaining was with the Powers that reside in each of these countries. And soon, I cam to understand many things which before I had no knowledge, except perhaps in dreams. The friends of my youth deserted me, and I them. When I was seven years gone from my family, I learned that they had all died of their own hand, for reasons no one was able to tell me; their flocks had been slain as the victims of some strange epidemic.

I wandered as a beggar, being fed from town to town as the local people saw fit, often being stoned instead and threatened with imprisonment. On occasion, I was able to convince some learned man that I was a sincere scholar, and was thereby permitted to read the ancient records in which the details of necromancy. sorcery, magick and alchemy are given. I learned of the spells that cause men illness, the plague, blindness, insanity, and even death. I learned of the various classes of demons and evil gods that exist, and of the old legends concerning the Ancient Ones. I was thus able to arm myself

against also the she-devil LAMMASHTA, who is called the Sword that Splits the Skull, the sight of whom causeth horror and dismay, and(some say) death of a most uncommon nature.

In time, I learned of the names and properties of all the demons, devils, fiends and monsters listed herein, in this Book of the Black Earth. I learned of the powers of the astral Gods, and how to summon their aid in times of need. I learned, too, of the frightful beings who dwell beyond the astral spirits, who guard the entrance to the Temple of the Lost, of the Ancient of Days, the Ancient of the Ancient Ones, whose Name I cannot write here.

In my solitary ceremonies in the hills, worshipping with fire and sword, with water and dagger, and with the assistance of a strange grass that grows wild in certain parts of

MASSHU, and with which I had unwittingly built my fire before the rock, that grass that gives the mind great power to travel tremendous distances into the heavens, as also into the hells, I received the formulae for the amulets and talismans which follow, which provide the Priest with safe passage among the spheres wherein he may travel in search of the Wisdom.

But now, after One Thousand-and-One moons of the journey, the Maskim nip at my heels, the Rabishu pull at my hair, Lammashta opens her dread jaws, AZAG-THOTH gloats blindly at his throne, KUTULU raises his head and stares up through the Veils of sunkun Varloorni, up through the Abyss, and fixes his stare upon me; wherefore I must with haste write this indeed, it appears as though I have failed in some regard as to the order of the rites, or to the formulae, or to the sacrifices, for now it appears as if the entire host of ERESHKIGAL lies waiting, dreaming, drooling for my departure. I pray the Gods that I am saved, and not perish as did the Priest, ABDUL BEN-MARTU, in Jerusalem (the Gods remember and have mercy upon him!). My fate is no longer writ in the stars, for I have broken the Chaldean Covenant by seeking power over the Zonei. I have set foot on the moon, and the moon no longer has power over me. The lines of my life have been oblitered by my wanderings in the Waste, over the letters writ in the heavens by the gods. And even now I can hear the wolves howling in the mountains as they did that fateful night, and they are calling my name, and the names of Others. I fear for my flesh, but I fear for my spirit more.

Remember, always, in every empty moment, to call upon the Gods not to forget thee, for they are forgetful and very far away. Light thy fires high in the hills, and on the tops of temples and pyramids, that they may see and remember.

Remember always to copy each of the formulae as I have put it down, and not to change it by one line or dot, not so much as a hair's breadth, lest it be rendered valueless, or worse: a broken star is the Gate of GANZIR, the Gate of Death, the Gate of the Shadows and the Shells. Recite the incantations as they are written here, in the manner this prescribed. Prepare the rituals without erring, and in the proper places and times render the sacrifices.

May the Gods be ever merciful unto thee!

May thou escape the jaws of the MASKIM, and vanquish the power of the Ancient Ones!

AND THE GODS GRANT THEE DEATH

BEFORE THE ANCIENT ONES RULE THE
EARTH ONCE MORE!

KAKAMMU! SELAH!

THE TESTIMONY OF THE MAD ARAB

(The Second Part)

UR! NIPPUR!

ERIDU! KULLAH!
KESH! LAGASH!
SHURUPPAL SELAH!

Day of Living, Rising Sun

Day of Plenty, gracious Sun
Day of Perfect, Grand Delight
Day of Fortune, Brilliant Night
O Shining Day!
O Laughing Day!
O Day of Life, and Love and Luck!
Seven Oldest, Wisest Ones!
Seven Sacred, Learned Ones!

Be my Guardians, polished Swords

Be my Watchful, patient Lords
Protect me from the Rabishu
O Shining, Splendorous APHKALLHU!

What God have I offended? What Goddess? What sacrifice have I failed to make? What Unknown Evil have I committed, that my going out should be thus accompanied by the fearful howlings of a hundred wolves?

May the heart of my God return to its place! May
the heart of my Goddess return to its place!

May the God I do not know be quieted toward me! May
the Goddess I do now know he quieted toward me!
May the heart of the Unknown God return to its place for me! May
the heart of the Unknown Goddess return to its place for me!

I have traveled on the Spheres, and the Spheres do not protect me. I have descended into the Abyss, and the Abyss does not protect me. I have walked to the tops of mountains, and the mountains do not protect me. I have walked the Seas, and the Seas do not protect me.

The Lords of the Wind rush about me and are angered. The Lords of the Earth crawl about my feet and are angered. The Spirits have forgotten me.

My time is shortened, and I must complete as much as I can before I am taken away by the Voice that ever calls. The Moon's days are numbered upon the earth, and the Sun's and I know not the meaning of these omens, but that they are. And the oracles are dried up, and the stars spin in their places. And the heavens look to be uncontrolled, with no order, and the spheres are crooked and wandering.

And the Sign of Zdaq is floating above my writing table, but I cannot read the runes any longer, for that Sight is failing me. Is it always in this fashion? And the Sign is failing me. Is it always in this fashion? And the Sign of Xastur rises up behind me, and of that I know the meaning, but may not write, for I received the message Elsewhere.

I can hardly speak to recognise my own voice.

The Abyss yawns wide before me! A gate has been broken!

Know that the Seven Spheres must be entered in their times and in their seasons, one at a time, and never the one before the other. Know that the Four beasts of the Spaces claim the blood of the initiate, each in their own time and season. Know that TIAMAT seeks ever to rise to the stars, and when the Upper is united to the Lower, then a new Age will come of Earth, and the Serpent shall be made whole, and the Waters will be as One, when on high the heavens had not been named.

Remember to protect the livestock of the village and thy family. The Elder Sign and the Sign of the Race. But the Watcher, too, if They be slow. And no sacrifices are to be made in that time, for the blood will be split for them that have come in, and will call them.

Remember to keep to the low ground, and not the high, for the Ancient Ones swing easily to the tops of the temples and the mountains, whereby they may survey what they had lost the last time. And sacrifices made on the tops of those temples are lost to Them.

Remember thy life is in running water, and not in still water, for the latter is the breeding place of the LILITU, and her creatures are the offspring of Them, and do worship at Their shrines, the places of which are unknown to thee. But where thou seest a standing stone, there they will be, for such is their altar.

Remember to carve the signs exactly as I have told thee, changing not one mark lest the amulet prove a curse against thee that wear it. Know that salt absorbs the evil effluvia of the larvae, and is useful to cleanse the tools with. Do not speak first to the demon, but let him speak first to thee. And is he speak, charge him to speak clearly, in a soft and pleasing voice, and in thy tongue, for it will otherwise surely confuse thee and deafen thee with its roar. And charge it to keep its stench that it may not make thee faint.

Remember not to make the sacrifice either too large or too small, for if it is too small, the demon will not come or, if coming, will be angered with thee so that it will not speak, even when charged, for that is the Covenant. And if it be too large, it will grow too large and too fast and will become difficult to control. And one such demon was raised by that Priest of Jerusalem, ABDUL BEN-MARTU, and was fed extensively on the sheep of the flocks of Palestine, whereupon it grew to frightening proportion and eventually devoured him. But that was madness, for Ben-Martu worshipped the Old Ones, which is unlawful, as it is written.

Remember that the Essences of the Ancient Ones are in all things, but that the Essences of the Elder Gods are in all things that live, and this will prove of value to thee when the time comes.

Remember the ARRA, especially when dealing with Them of Fire, for They respect it, and no other.

Remember to keep the Moon pure.

Beware of the Cults of Death, and these are the Cult of the Dog, the Cult of the Dragon, and the Cult of the Goat; for they are worshippers of the Ancient Ones, and forever try to let Them in, for they have a formulae of which it is unlawful to speak. And these cults are not strong, save at their seasons, when the heavens open up to them and unto their race.

And there shall forever be War between us and the Race of Draconis, for the Race of Draconis was ever powerful in ancient times, when the first temples were built in MAGAN, and they drew down much strength from the stars, but now they are as

Wanderers of the Wastelands, and dwell in caves and in deserts, and in all lonely places where they have set up stones. And these I have seen, in my journeys through those areas where the ancient cults once flourished, and where now there is only sadness and desolation.

And I have seen them in their Rites, and the awful Things they call forth from the Lands beyond Time. I have seen the Signs carved upon their stones, their altars. I have seen the Sign of PAZUZU, and ZALED, and those of XASTUR and AZAG-THOTH, and similarly those of ISHNIGARRAB and the awful Offspring of the Goat, and the terrible musicks of their Race.

I have seen the Blood split upon the Stone. I have seen that Stone struck with a Sword, and have seen the Stone raise up and the Serpent crawl forth. And this power is surely damned; but where does MARDUK tarry? And what of SHAMMASH? The Sleeping Gods truly Sleep.

And what crime have I committed? What Unknown God have I transgressed? What forbidden thing have I eaten? What forbidden thing have I drunk? My suffering! It is Seven! It is Seven times Seven! O Gods! Do not cast thy servant down!

Remember the Scorpion Man who dwells in the Mountains. He was of old created by TIAMAT to fight the Elder Gods, but was permitted to stay below the Mountains by Them. But He has deceived us once, and may do so again. But call upon him if there be something concerning the Outside that you would know, that I have not told thee. And his sign is simple, and it is thus:

And merely, face the place where he is, and he will come and speak, but do not do this at Dawn, for then the Sun rises and the Scorpion has no power, not from the Dawn till the Dusk, during which time he is forced back beneath the Earth, for that is the letter of the Covenant concerning him, for it is written: He shall not raise his head above the Sun.

And again: His is the dark times.

And again: He knows of the Gate, but not the Gate

And the Scorpion Man has another of his Race, female, that dwells with him there, but of her it is not lawful to speak, and she must be banished with the exorcisms should she appear to thee, for her touch is Death.

And of the Cult of the Dragon, what more can I say to thee? They worship when that Star is highest in the heavens, and is of the Sphere of the IGIGI, as are the Stars of the Dog and the Goat. And their worshippers have always been with us, though they are not of our same Race, but of the Race of their Stars, of the Ancient Ones. And they keep not to our laws, but murder quickly, and without thought. And their blood covers them.

They have summoned the Spirits of War and Plague openly upon our Race, and have caused great numbers of our people and our animals die, after a most unnatural fashion.

And they are unfeeling towards pain, and fear not the Sword or the Flame, for they are the authors of all Pain! They are the very creatures of Darkness and Sorrow, yet they Sorrow not! Remember the smell! They can be told by their smell! And their many unnatural sciences and arts, which cause wonderous things to happen, but which are unlawful to our people.

And who is their Master? Of this I do not know, but I have heard them calling ENKI which is surely a blasphemy, for ENKI is of our Race as it is writ in the Text of MAGAN. But, perhaps, they called Another, whose Name I do not know. But surely it was not ENKI.

And I have heard them calling all the Names of the Ancient Ones, proudly, at their Rites. And I have seen the blood split upon the ground and the mad dancing and the terrible cries as they yelled upon their Gods to appear and aid them in their mysteries.

And I have seen them turn the very Moon's rays into liquid, the which they poured upon their stones for a purpose I could not divine.

And I have seen them turn into many strange kinds of beast as they gathered in their appointed places, the Temples of Offal, whereupon horns grew from heads that had not horns, and teeth from mouths that had not such teeth, and hands become as the talons of eagles or the claws of dogs that roam the desert areas, mad and howling, like unto those who even now call my name outside this room!

I cry laments, but no one hears me! I am overwhelmed with horror! I cannot see! Gods, do not cast thy servant down!

Remember the Sword of the Watcher. Do not touch It until you want It to depart, for It will depart at a touch and leave thee unprotected for the remainder of the Rite, and although a Circle is a boundary which none can cross, thou wilt find thyself unprepared to meet the incredible sights that will greet thee outside.

Remember also the sacrifices to the Watcher. They must be regular, for the Watcher is of a different Race and cares not for thy life, save that he obey thy commands when the

sacrifices have been met.

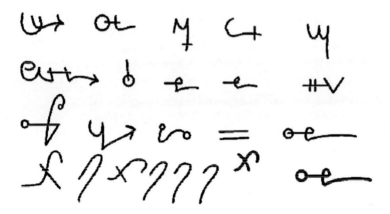

And forgetting the Elder Sign will surely cause thee much grief.

And I have seen a Race of Man that worships a Giant Cow. And they come from somewhere East, beyond the Mountains. And they are surely worshippers of an Ancient One, but of its Name I am not certain, and do not write it down, for it is useless to thee anyway. And in their Rites, they become as cows, and it is disgusting to see. But they are Evil, and so I warn thee.

And I have seen Rites that can kill a man at a great distance. And Rites that can cause sickness to a man, wherever he lives, by the use of a simple charm, which must be spoken in its tongue and in no other, or so it is said. And this charm is as follows:

AZAG galra sagbi mu unna te

NAMTAR galra zibi mu unna te
UTUK XUL gubi mu unna te
ALA XUL gabi mu unna te
GIDIM XUL ibbi mu unna te
GALLA XUL kadbi mu unna te
DINGIR XUL girbi mu unna te
I minabi-ene tashbi aba aba-andibbi-esh!

And this they would chant over a doll of wax as it was burning in their wicked cauldrons. And in these things they took great delight, and still do where they are to be found at their shrines of loathsomeness.

And I have seen the lands of farmers ravaged by their evil spells, scorched black by flame and burning embers that descend from the sky. And that is the Sign that they have been there, where the earth is black and charred, and where nothing grows.

And when fire comes from the heavens, there wilt surely be panic among the people, and the Priest must calm them an take this book, of which he must make a copy in his own, and read the exorcisms therein that his people may not be harmed. For a sword will appear in the sky at those times, a signal to the Ancient Ones that One of Theirs has escaped and entered into this World. And it shall be an omen to thee that such a Spirit is abroad in the land, and must be found. And thou mayest send thy Watcher to the search, and it will be great destruction of cities, and fire will rain from the spheres, until the Elder Gods see your plight and will quell the uprising of the Ancient Ones with powerful Charms. But many will be lost to the Outside at that time.

Watch well the Stars. For when comets are to be seen in the neighbourhood of CAPRICORNUS, His cults will rejoice and the spells will increase from their quarter. And when comets are to be seen in DRACONIS, there is a great danger, for the Cults of the Dragon do rise up at that time, and make many sacrifices, not only of animals, but of men.

And when comets are to be seen in the neighborhood of the Star SIRIUS, then there will be great difficulty in the house of kings, and brother will rise up against brother, and there shall be war and famine. And in these things the worshippers of the Dog will rejoice, and reap the spoils of these conflicts, and will grow fat.

If thou happenest upon such a Cult in the midst of their Rituals, do but hide well so that they do not see thee, else they will surely kill thee and make of thee a sacrifice to their Gods, and thy spirit will be in grave danger, and the howling of the wolves will be for thee and the spirit which escapes from thee. This, if thou be lucky to die quickly, for these Cults rejoice in the slow spilling of blood, whereby they derive much power and strength in their Ceremonies.

Watch well, however, all that they do and all that they say, and write it down in a book that no one will see, as I have done, for it will serve thee well at some future time when thou wilt recognize them by their words or by their actions. And thou mayest procure amulets against them, by which their spells are rendered useless and dull, by burning the Name of their Gods upon parchment or silk in a cauldron of thine own devising. And thy Watcher will carry the burnt spell to their altar and deposit it thereupon, and they will be much afraid and cease their workings for awhile, and their stones will crack and their Gods be sorely angry with their servants.

Write the book thou keepest well, and clearly, and when it is time for thee to go out, as it is my time now, it will pass into the hands of those who may have the best use of it, and who are faithful servants of the Elder Gods, and wilt swear eternal Warfare against the

rebellious demons who would destroy the civilisations of man.

And if thou knowest the names of they who would harm thee, write them upon figures of wax, made in their image, upon which you will make the Curse and melt them in the cauldron you have set up within the MANDAL of protection. And the Watcher will carry the Curse to them for whom it was uttered. And they will die.

And if thou does not know of their names, nor of their persons, save that they seek to harm thee, make a doll of wax like a man, with his limbs, but with no face. And upon the face of the doll write the word KASHSHAPTI. Hold the doll over the flaming cauldron while saying fiercely over it:

ATTI MANNU KASHSHAPTU SHA TUYUB TA ENNI!

and then drop the doll into the flame. From the smoke that rises from this action, you will see the name of the sorcerer or sorceress written within it. And then you will be able to send the Watcher to bring the Curse. And that person will die.

Or thou mayest call upon ISHTAR to protect thee from the spells of sorcery. And for this, the MANDAL must be prepared as always, and a figure of ISHTAR be upon the altar, and incantations made to summon Her assistance, like the following incantation that is ancient, from the Priests of UR:

WHO ART THOU, O WITCH, THAT SEEKEST ME?

Thou hast taken the road
Thou hast come after me
Thou hast sought me continually for my destruction
Thou hast continually plotted an evil thing against me
Thou hast encompassed me
Thou hast sought me out
Thou hast gone forth and followed my steps

But I, by the command of the Queen ISHTAR

Am clothed in terror
Am armed in fiercesomeness
Am arrayed with might and the Sword
I make thee tremble
I make thee run afraid

I drive thee out
I spy thee out
I cause thy name to be known among men
I cause they house to be seen amoung men
I cause thy spells to be heard amoung men
I cause thy evil perfumes to be smelt amoung men

I unclothe thy wickedness and evil

And bring your sorceries to naught!

It is not I, but NANAKANISURRA

Mistress of Witches
And the Queen of heaven ISHTAR
Who command thee!

And if these worshippers and sorcerers still come at thee, as it is possible, for their power comes from the Stars, and who knows the ways of the Stars?, thou must call upon the Queen of Mysteries, NINDINUGGA, who wilt surely save thee. And thou must make incantations with her Title, which is NINDINUGGA NIMSHIMSHARGAL ENLILLARA. And it is enough merely to shout that Name aloud, Seven times, and she will come to thine aid.

And remember that thou purify thy temple with the branches of cypress and of pine, and no evil spirit which haunteth buildings will cause habitation to be set up therein, and no larvae will breed, as they do in many unclean places. The larvae are enormous, twice as large as a man, but do breed on his excretions, and even, it s said, upon his breath, and grow to terrible height, and do not leave him until the Priest or some magician cut him off with the copper dagger, saying the name of ISHTAR seven times seven times, aloud, in a sharp voice.

The night has now grown silent. The howling of the wolves has grown quiet, and can scarce be heard. Perhaps it was some other that they sought? Yet, can I tell in my bones that this is not so? For the XASTUR sign has not left its station behind me, and has grown larger, casting a shadow over these pages as I write. I have summoned my Watcher, but It is troubled by some Things and does not respond to me well, as though afflicted with some disease, and dazed.

My books have lost light, and settle upon their shelves like animals fallen asleep, or dead. I am sickened by what voices I hear now, as though the voices of my family, left behind me so many years ago, that is impossible to conceive that they are about. Did I not understand of their untimely, unnatural death? Can the demons who wait Without take on so viciously the human voices of my parents? My brother? My sister?

AVAUNT THEE!

That this Book were an amulet, a Seal of Protection! That my ink were the ink of Gods and not of Men! But I must write hastily, and if thou cannot read nor understand this writing, perhaps it is sign enough for thee of the strength and power of the demons that be, in these times and in these places, and is surely a warning to thee to have a care and not to invoke carelessly, but cautiously, and not, under any circumstances, seek carelessly to open that Gate to the Outside, for thou can never know the Seasons of Times of the Ancient Ones, even though thou can tell their Seasons upon the Earth by the rules I have already instructed thee to compute; for their Times and Seasons Outside run uneven and

strange to our minds, for are they not the Computors of All Time? Did they not set Time in its Place? It were not enough that the Elder Gods (have mercy on Thy servant!) set the Wanderers to mark their spaces, for such spaces as existed were the work of the Ancient Ones. Were no Sun to shine, were SHAMMASH never born, would not the years pass by, as quickly?

Seek ever to keep the Outside Gate closed and sealed, by the instructions I have given thee, by the Seals and the Names herein.

Seek ever to hold back the Powers of the Cults of the ancient Worship, that they might not grow strong on their blood, and on their sacrifice. By their wounds shall ye know them, and by their smell, for they are not born as men, but in some other fashion; by some corruption of seed or spirit that has given them other properties than those we are familiar with. And they like the Dark Places best; for their God is a Worm.

IA! SHADDUYA IA! BARRA! BARRA! IA KANPA! IA KANPA!
ISHNIGARRAB! IA! NNGI IA! IA!

The Stars grow dim in their places, and the Moon pales before me, as though a Veil were blown across its flame. Dog-faces demons approach the circumference of my sanctuary. Strange lines appear carved on my door and walls, and the light from the Windows grows increasing dim.

A wind has risen. The Dark Waters stir. This is the Book of the Servant of the Gods . .

OF THE ZONEI AND THEIR ATTRIBUTES

THE Gods of the Stars are Seven. They have Seven Seals, each of which may be used in their turn. They are approached by Seven Gates, each of which may be opened in their turn. They have Seven Colours, Seven Essences, and each a separate Step on the Ladder of Lights. The Chaldeans were but imperfect in their knowledge, although they had understanding of the Ladder, and certain of the formulae. They did not, however, possess the formulae for the passing of the Gates, save one, of whom it is forbidden to speak.

The passing of the Gates gives the priest both power and wisdom to use it. He becomes able to control the affairs of his life more perfectly than before, and many have been content to merely pass the first three Gates and then sit down and go no further than that, enjoying the benefits that they have found on the preliminary spheres. But this is Evil, for they are not equipped to deal with the attack from Without that must surely come, and their people will cry unto them for safety, and it will not come forth. Therefore, set thy face towards the ultimate goal and strive ever onward to the furthest reaches of the stars, though it mean thine own death; for such a death is as a sacrifice to the Gods, and pleasing, that they will not forget their people.

The ZONEI and their attributes, then, are as follows:

The God of the Moon is the God NANNA. He is Father of the Zonei, and the Eldest of the Wanderers. He is long of beard, and bears a wand of lapis lazuli in his palm, and possesses the secret of the tides of blood. His colour is Silver. His Essence is to be found in Silver, and in camphor, and in those things bearing the sign of the Moon. He is sometimes called SIN. His Gate is the first you will pass in the rituals that follow. His

Step on the Ladder of Lights is also Silver.

This is his Seal, which you must engrave on his metal, on the thirteenth day of the Moon in which you are working, having no other person about you who may watch you in its manufacture. Being finished, it should be wrapped in a square of the finest silk and lain aside until such time as you desire its use, and then, it should be removed only after the Sun has gone to its rest. No ray of sunlight should strike the Seal, lest its power be rendered nil and a new Seal must needs be cast.

The Number of NANNA is Thirty and this is his Seal:

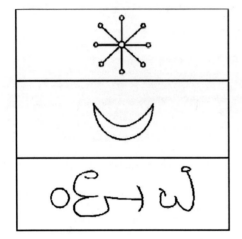

The God of Mercury is NEBO. He is a very old spirit, having a long beard, and is the guardian of the Gods, as well as the keeper of the knowledge of Science. He wears a crown of one hundred horns, and the long robe of the Priest. His colour is blue. His Essence is in that metal known as Quicksilver, and is sometimes also found in sand, and in those things bearing the sign of Mercury. His Gate is the Second you will pass in the rituals that follow. His Step on the Ladder of Lights is blue.

This is his Seal, which you must write on perfect parchment, or no the broad leaf of a palm tree, having no other person about you who may watch you in its construction. Being finished, it should be wrapped in a square of the finest silk and lain aside until such time as you desire its use, and then, it should be removed only when its light is in the sky. Such is also the best time for its manufacture.

The Number of NEBO is Twelve and this is his Seal:

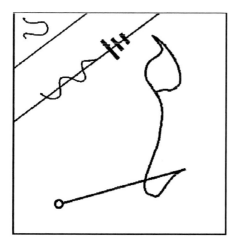

The Goddess of Venus is the most excellent Queen INANNA, called of the Babylonians ISHTAR. She is the Goddess of Passion, both of Love and of War, depending upon her sign and the time of her appearance in the heavens. She appears as a most beautiful Lady, in the company of lions, and partakes of a subtle astral nature with the Moon God NANNA. When they are in agreement, that is, when their two plants are auspiciously arranged in the heavens, it is as two offering-cups split freely in the heavens, to rain the sweet wine of the Gods upon the earth. And then there is great happiness and rejoicing. She sometimes appears in armour, and is thereby a most excellent guardian against the machinations of her sister, the dread Queen ERESHKIGAL of KUR. With the Name and Number of INANNA, no Priest need fear to walk into the very depths of the Underworld; for being armed, in Her armour, he is similar to the Goddess. It was thus that I descended into the foul pits that lie gaping beneath the crust of the earth, and commanded demons.

She is similarly the Goddess of Love, and bestows a favourable bride upon any man who desires it, and who makes the proper sacrifice.

BUT KNOW THAT INANNA TAKES HER OWN FOR HER OWN, AND THAT ONCE CHOSEN BY HER NO MAN MAY TAKE ANOTHER BRIDE.

Her colour is the purest White. Her manifestation is in the metal Copper, and also in the most beautiful flowers of a field, and in the saddest death of the battlefield, which is that field's fairest flower. Her Gate is the Third you will pass in the rites that follow, and in which place you will be of a heart to stay; but turn you face to the road that leads beyond, for that is your genuine goal, unless the Goddess choses you. Her Step on the Ladder of Lights, built of old in Babylon and at UR, is White.

This is her Seal, which you must engrave on Copper, Venus being exalted in the Heavens, with no one about watching its construction. Being finished, it is to be wrapped in the purest silk and lain safely away, only to be removed when need arises, at any time.

The Number of INANNA is Fifteen, by which Number she is frequently known in the incantations of the Dispensation, her Seal is the following.

This God of the Sun is the Lord SHAMMASH, son of NANNA. He is seated upon a throne of gold, wearing a crown of two horns, holding a sceptre aloft in his right hand

and a flame disk in his life, sending rays in every direction. He is the God of Light and of life. His colour is Gold. His Essence is to be found in gold, and in all golden objects and plants. He is sometimes called UDUU. His Gate is the Fourth you will pass in the rituals that follow. His Step on the great Ladder of Lights is Gold.

This is his Seal, which you must engrave in gold, when the Sun is exalted in the heavens, alone on a mountain top or some such place close to the Rays, but alone. Being finished, it should be wrapped in a square of the finest silk and lain aside until such time as it is needed.

The Number os SHAMMASH is Twenty and this is his Seal:

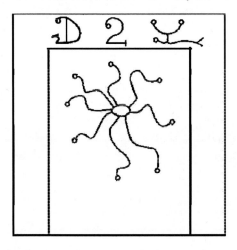

The God of Mars is the mighty NERGAL.

He has the head of a man on the body of a lion, and bears a sword and a flail. He is the God of War, and of the fortunes of War. He was sometimes though to be an agent of the Ancient Ones, for he dwelt in CUTHA for a time. His colour is dark red. His essence is to be found in Iron, and in all weapons made to spill the blood of men and of animals. His Gate is the Fifth you will see as you pass the Zones in the rituals that follow. His Step on the Ladder of Light is Red.

This is his Seal, which must be engraved on a plate of Iron, or on paper in blood, when Mars is in exaltation in the heavens. It is best done at night, far from the habitations of men and of animals, where you cannot be seen or heard. It must be wrapped first in heavy cloth, then in fine silk, and hid safe away until such times as it is needed. But to take not to use this Seal hastily, for it is a sharp Sword.

The Number of NERGAL is Eight and this is his Seal:

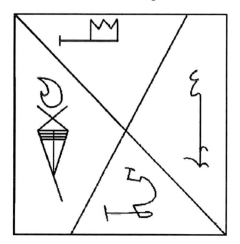

The God of Jupiter is the Lord of Magicians, MARDUK KURIOS of the Double-headed Axe. MARDUK was born of our Father, ENKI, to do battle against the forces of the Ancient Ones, and he won a powerful fight, subduing the armies of Evil and putting the Queen of the Ancient Ones beneath his foot. That Serpent is dead, but dreams. MARDUK was bestowed Fifty Names and Powers by the Council of the Elder Gods, which Powers he retains to this day. His colour is Purple. His Essence is in the material tin, and in brass. His Gate is the Sixth that you will come upon as you follow the rituals that follow. His Step on the Ladder of Lights in Purple.

This is his Seal, which you must engrave on a plate of tin or of brass, when Jupiter is strong in the heavens, while making special invocation to ENKI Our Master. This shall be wrought as the others, and wrapped in pure silk and lain away until the time for its use. Know that MARDUK appears as a mighty warrior with a long beard and a flaming disk in his hands. He carries a bow and a quiver of arrows, and treads about the heavens keeping the Watch. Take care to summon his assistance in only the most terrible of circumstances, for his might is powerful and his anger fierce. When thou hast need of the power of the star Jupiter, call instead one of the appropriate Powers listed within these pages, and they will surely come.

The Number of Marduk is Ten and this is his Seal:

The God of Saturn is NINIB called ADAR, the Lord of Hunters and of Strength. He appears with a crown of horns and a long sword, wearing a lion's skin. he is the final Zonei before the terrible IGIGI. His colour is the darkest black. His Essence is to be found in lead, in the burnt embers of the fire, and in things of death and of antiquity. The horns of a stag are his symbol. His Gate is the Last you will come upon in the rites that follow. His Step on the Ladder of Lights is Black.

This is his Seal, which you must engrave on a leaden plate or bowl, keeping it well hidden from the eyes of the profane. It should be wrapped and put away as all the others, until its use is desired. It should never be removed when the Sun is in the sky, but only after the night has fallen and the earth grown black, for NINIB knows the best the ways of the demons that prowl among the shadows, looking for sacrifice. he knows best the territories of the Ancient Ones, the practices of their worshippers, and the locations of the Gates. His realm is the realm of the Night of Time.

His Number is Four, as the quarters of the Earth, and the following is his Seal:

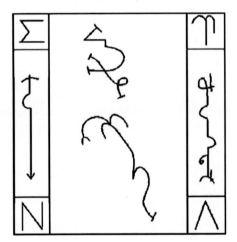

THE BOOK OF ENTRANCE, AND OF THE WALKING

THE BOOK OF ENTRANCE

THIS is the Book of Entrance to the Seven Zones above the Earth, which Zones were known to the Chaldeans, and to the ancient races that preceded them among the lost temples of UR. Know that these Zones are governed by the celestial spirits, and that passage may be had by the Priest through those lands that border on the Unzoned Wastes beyond. Know that, when Walking thus through the Sea of Spheres, he should leave his Watcher behind that It may guard his body and his property, lest he be slain unawares and must wander throughout eternity among the dark spaces between Stars, or else be devoured by the wrathful IGIGI that dwell beyond.

Know that thou must Walk the Steps of the Ladder of Lights, each in its place and one at a time, and that thou must enter by the Gates in the lawful manner, as is put down in the Covenant; else thou art surely lost.

Know that thou must keep purified for the space of one moon for the Entrance to the first Step, one moon between the First and the Second Step, and again between the Second and the Third, and so on in like manner. Thou must abstain from spilling thy seed in any manner for like period of time, but thou mayest worship at the Temple of ISHTAR,

provided thou lose not thine Essence. And this is a great secret.

Thou must needs call upon thy God in the dawn light and upon thy Goddess in the light of dusk, every day of the moon of purification. Thou must summon thy Watcher and instruct it perfectly in its duties, providing it with a time and a place whereby it may serve thee and surround thee with a flaming sword, in every direction.

Thy clothing for the Walking should be fair, clean and simple, but appropriate to each Step. And thou should have with thee the Seal of the particular Step whereupon thou Walkest, which is the Seal of the Star appertaining thereunto.

Thou must needs prepare an alter to face the North, having upon it the statues of thine deities, or some such suitable Images, an offering bowl, and a brazier. Upon the earth should be inscribed the Gate appropriate to the Walking. If above thee is the Sky, so much the better. If there be a roof above thine head, it must be free from all hangings. Not even a lamp should be suspended over thee, save in Operations of Calling, which is discussed elsewhere (if the Gods grant me the time!). The only light shall be from the four lamps upon the ground, at each of the four Gates of the Earth: of the North, one lamp; pf the East, one lamp; of the South, one lamp; and of the West, one lamp. The oil should be pure, with no odour, or else sweet-smelling. The perfumes in the brazier should also be sweet-smelling, or especially appropriate to the Star where thou wouldst desire Entrance, after the fashion of thy country.

The Seven Gates here follow:

THIS IS THE FIRST GATE THE GATE OF NANNA, CALLED SIN:

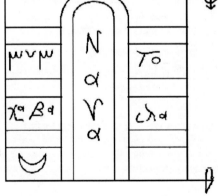

THIS IS THE SECOND GATE, OF NEBO:

THIS IS THE THIRD GATE, OF INANNA CALLED ISHTAR:

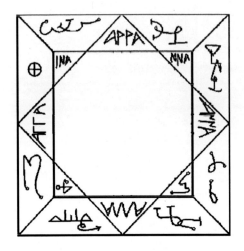

THIS IS THE FOURTH GATE, OF SHAMMASH, CALLED UDDU:

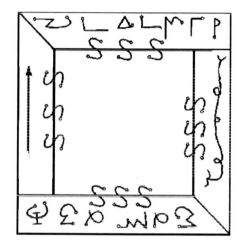

THIS IS THE FIFTH GATE, OF NERGAL:

THIS IS THE SIXTH GATE, OF LORD MARDUK:

THIS IS THE SEVENTH GATE, OF NINIB, CALLED ADAR:

And the Ritual of the Walking must follow the formulae herein described:

First, thou must observe the moon of purification. In this time, thou mayest not eat meat for the space of seven days preceding the last day of the moon, and for the space of three days preceding the last dat of the moon thou mayest not eat anything whatsoever, save to drink sweet water. On the last three days, thou must invoke, in addition to thy God and

Goddess, the Three Great Elder Ones, ANU, ENLIL, ENKI, by their proper invocations. And the Number of ANU is Sixty, the Perfect Number, for he is Father of the Heavens. And the Number of ENLIL is Fifty, and he is the Father of the Wind. And the Number of ENKI is Forty a most excellent Number, and he is our Father, of all who would tread these forgotten paths, and wander into Lands unknown, among the Wastes, amid frightful monsters of the Azonei.

Second, on the Night of the Walking, which must be the thirteenth night of the moon, having begun on the previous thirteenth night, thou must approach the Gate with awe and respect. Thy Temple is exorcised. Thou must light the Fire and conjure it, but the invocation of the God of Fire, and pour incense thereon. Thou must make offering to the Deities on the altar.

Third, thou must light the four lamps from the flaming brazier, reciting the invocation proper to each of these Watchtowers in its proper place, summoning the respective Star.

Fourth , thou must recite the invocation of the Watcher, thrusting the Sword into the Earth at Its station, not touching it until it is the appointed time for Its departure.

Fifth , thou must take the Seal of the Star in thy right hand, and whisper its Name softly upon it.

Sixth, thou must recite the Incantation of the Walking, loudly, and in a clear voice, as thou walkest about the Gate in a circular fashion, beginning at the North and walking to the East, then to the South, and to the West, the Number of turns being equal to the special Number of the Star.

Seventh, thou must needs arrive back at the centre of the Gate, before thine altar, at which time thou must fall to the ground, looking neither to the right no to the left at what may be moving there, for these Operations attract many kinds of wandering demon and ghost to the Gates, but in the air above the altar whereupon thou wilt presently see the Gate opening for thee and the Spirit-Messenger of the Sphere greeting thee in a clear voice, and giving thee a Name, which thou must remember, for that is the Name of thy Passing the Gate, which thou must use each time thou passeth thereby. The same Spirit-messenger will meet thee and, if thou know not thy Name, he will forbid thee entrance and thou wilt fall to the Earth immediately.

When the First Gate has been entered and the Name received, thou wilt fall back to Earth amid thine Temple. That which has been moving about thy Gate on the ground will have gone. Recite thine thanksgiving to the Gods upon thine altar, strike the Sword of the Watcher that It may depart, and give the incantation of INANNA which say how she conquered the realm of the Underworld and vanquisheth KUTULU. All Idimmu will vanish thereby and thou wilt be thus free to depart the Gate and extinguish the Fire.

Thou mayest not call upon NANNA till thou hast passed the Gate of NANNA. Thou mayest not call NEBO until his Gate hast thou passed. Similarly for the rest of the Gates. When thou hast ascended to the limit of the Ladder of Lights, thou wilt have knowledge and power over the Spheres, and wilt be able to summon them thereby in times of need. This will not give thee power over the ABSU, however, this power being obtained differently by the Ritual of Descent. This Ritual thou wilt undertake in the fifteenth day after the thirteenth of the month when thou hast summoned the Gate of MARDUK to open. For MARDUK slew the Fiends, and INANNA, the Goddess of the Fifteen, conquered the Netherworld, where some of theirs still dwell. This is a most perilous Rite, and may be undertaken by any man who as the formulae, whether he has passes the previous Gates or not, save that it is best advised to have passed through MARDUK Gate before venturing forth into the Pit. For this reason, few have ever opened the Gate of ADAR, and spoken to the Horned One who resideth there and giveth all manner of wisdom regarding the operations of necromancy, and of the spells that hasten unto death. Only when thou hast shown thy power over the Maskim and the Rabishu, mayest thou venture forth to the Land of the IGIGI, and for that reason was this Covenant made, that none shall safely Walk through the sunken valleys of the Dead before having ascended to MARDUK, nor shall they breach the Gates that lie beyond ADAR until they have seen the Signs of the Mad God and felt the fury of the hellish Queen.

And against the Ancient Ones, there is only defence. Only a madman, indeed, such as I am called!, can hope to have power over Them that dwell in the Outer Spaces, for their power is unknown, and the number of the hordes uncounted, and each day they breed more horrors than a man's mind can conceive, the sight of which he can hardly bear. There was a time when the Gate to the Outside was open too long and I witnessed the horror that struck, of which words cannot speak, and of which writing can only confuse. The Ancient One that had escaped into the Inner World was forced back through the Gate by a magician of great power, but only at a great loss to the villages and flocks of the Island. Many sheep were slain after an unnatural fashion, and many devoured, an many Bedou rendered senseless; for the mind perceives what it is shown, but the sight of the Ancient Ones is a blasphemy to the ordinary senses of a man, for that come from a world that is not straight, but crooked, and their existence is of forms unnatural and painful to the eye and to the mind, whereby the spirit is threatened and wrenches loose from the body in flight. And for that reason, the fearful utukku xul take possession of the body and dwell therein until the Priest banish them back to whence they came, and the normal spirit may return to its erstwhile neighbourhood.

And there are all the ALLU, frightening dog-faced demons that are the Messengers of the Gods of Prey, and that chew on the very bones of man. And there are many another, of which this is not the rightful place wherein they may be mentioned, save to warn the Priest against the ambitious striving against the Ancient Ones of the Outside, until mastery is acquired over the powers that reside Within. Only when ADAR has been obtained, may the Priest consider himself a master of the planes of the Spheres, and able to wrestle with the Old Gods. Once Death Herself has been stared in the Eye, can the Priest then summon and control the denizens of Death's darkly curtained halls. Then can he hope to open the Gate without fear and without that loathing of the spirit that slays the

man.

Then cane he hope to have power over the demons that plague the mind and the body, pulling at the hair and grasping at the hands, and the screaming vile Names into the airs of the Night.

For what comes on the Wind can only be slain by he who knows the Wind; and what comes on the seas can only be slain by he who knows the Waters. This is it written, in the Ancient Covenant.

THE INCANTATIONS OF THE GATES

THE INVOCATION OF THE NANNA GATE

Spirit of the Moon, Remember!

NANNA, Father of the Astral Gods, Remember!
In the Name of the Covenant sworn between Thee and the Race of Men,
I call to Thee! Hearken, and Remember!
From the Gates of the Earth, I call Thee! From the Four Gates of the Land KI, I pray to Thee!
O Lord, Hero of the Gods, who in heaven and upon the earth is exalted!
Lord NANNA, of the Race of ANU, hear me!
Lord NANNA, called SIN, hear me!
Lord NANNA, Father of the Gods of UR, hear me!
Lord NANNA, God of the Shining Crown of Night, hear me!

Maker of Kings, Progenitor of the Land, Giver of the Gilded Sceptre,
Hear me and Remember!
Mighty Father, Whose thought is beyond the comprehension of gods and men,
Hear me and Remember!
Gate of the Great Gates of the Spheres, open unto me!
Master of the IGIGI, swing open Thy Gate!
Master of the ANNUNAKI, open the Gate to the Stars!
IA NAMRASIT! IA SIN! IA NANNA!
BASTAMAAGANASTA IA KIA KANPA!
MAGABATHI-YA NANNA KANPA!
MASHRITA NANNA ZIA KANPA!
IA MAG! IA GAMAG! IA ZAGASTHENA KIA!
ASHTAG KARELLIOSH!

THE INVOCATION OF THE NEBO GATE

Spirit of the Swift Planet, Remember!
NEBO, Custodian of the Gods, Remember!

NEBO, Father of the Sacred Writing, Remember!
In the Name of the Covenant sworn between Thee and the Race of Men, I
call to Thee! Hearken, and Remember!
From the Gate of the Great God NANNA, I call to Thee!
By the Name which I was given on the Lunar Sphere, I call to Thee!
Lord NEBO, who does not know of Thy Wisdom?
Lord NEBO, who does not know of Thy Magick?
Lord NEBO, what spirit, on earth or in heavens, is not conjured by Thy mystic Writing?
Lord NEBO, what spirit, on earth or in the heavens, is not compelled by the Magick of
Thy spells?
NEBO KURIOS! Lord of the Subtle Arts, Open the Gate to the Sphere of Thy Spirit!
NEBO KURIOS! Master of the Chemical Science, Open the Gate to the Sphere of Thy
Workings!
Gate of the Swift Planet, MERKURIOS, Open unto me!
IA ATHZOTHTU! IA ANGAKU! IA ZI NEBO!
MARZAS ZI FORNIAS KANPA!
LAZHAKAS SHIN TALAS KANPA!
NEBOS ATHANATOS KANPA!

IA GAASH! IA SAASH! IA KAKOLOMANI-YASH!
IA MAAKALLI!

THE INVOCATION OF THE ISHTAR GATE

Spirit of Venus, Remember!

ISHTAR, Mistress of the Gods, Remember!
ISHTAR, Queen of the Land of the Rising of the Sun, Remember!
Lady of Ladies, Goddess of Goddesses, ISHTAR, Queen of all People, Remember!
O Bright Rising, Torch of the Heaven and of the Earth, Remember!
O Destroyer of the Hostile Hordes, Remember! Lioness,
Queen of the Battle, Hearken and Remember! From the
Gate of the Great God NEBO, I call Thee!

By the Name which I was given on the Sphere of NEBO, I call to Thee!
Lady, Queen of Harlots and of Soldiers, I call to Thee!
Lady, Mistress of Battle and of Love, I pray Thee, Remember!
In the Name of the Covenant, sworn between Thee and the Race of Men, I
call to Thee! Hearken and Remember!
Suppressor of the Mountains!
Supporter of arms!

Deity of Men! Goddess of Women! Where Thou gazest, the Dead live!
ISHTAR, Queen of Night, Open Thy Gate to me!

ISHTAR, Lady of the Battle, Open wide Thy Gate!
ISHTAR, Sword of the People, Open Thy Gate to me!
ISHTAR, Lady of the Gift of Love, Open wide Thy Gate!
Gate of the Gentle Planet, LIBAT, Open unto me!
IA GUSHE-YA! IA INANNA! IA ERNINNI-YA!
ASHTA PA MABACHA CHA KUR ENNI-YA!
RABBMI LO-YAK ZI ISHTARI KANPA!
INANNA ZI AMMA KANPA! BI ZAMMA KANPA!
IA IA IA BE-YI RAZULUKI!

THE INVOCATION OF THE SHAMMASH GATE

Spirit of the Sun, Remember!

SHAMMASH, Lord of the Fiery Disk, Remember!
In the Name of the Covenant sworn between Thee and Race of Men,
I call to Thee! Hearken and Remember!
From the Gate of the Beloved ISHTAR, the Sphere of LIBAT, I call to Thee! Illuminator
of Darkness, Destroyer of Evil, Lamp of Wisdom, I call to Thee! SHAMMASH, Bringer

of Light, I call to Thee! KUTULU is burned by Thy Might! AZAG-THOTH is fallen off
His Throne before Thee! ISHNIGARRAB is scorched black by Thy rays!
Spirit of the Burning Disk, Remember! Spirit
of the Never-Ending Light, Remember!

Spirit of the Rending of the Veils of the Night, Dispeller of Darkness, Remember!
Spirit of the Opening of the Day, Open wide Thy Gate!
Spirit Who rises between the Mountains with splendour, Open Thy Gate to me! By
the Name which I was given on the Sphere of ISHTAR, I ask Thy Gate to open!
Gate of the Sun, Open to me!
Gate of the Golden Sceptre, Open to me!
Gate of the Life-Giving Power, Open! Open!
IA UDDU-YA! IA RUSSULUXI!
SAGGTAMARANIA! IA! IA! ATZARACHI-YA!
ATZARELECHI-YU! BARTALAKATAMANI-YA KANPA!

ZI DINGIR UDDU-YA KANPA! ZI DINGIR USHTU-YA KANPA!
ZI SHTA! ZI DARAKU! ZI BELURDUK!
KANPA! IA SHTA KANPA! IA!

THE INVOCATION OF THE NERGAL GATE

Spirit of the Red Planet, Remember!

NERGAL, God of War, Remember!

NERGAL, Vanquisher of Enemies, Commander of Hosts, Remember!
NERGAL, Slayer of Lions and of Men, Remember!
In the Name of the Covenant sworn between Thee and the Race of Men, I call
to Thee! Hearken and Remember!
From the Great Gate of the Lord SHAMMASH, the Sphere of the Sun, I call
to Thee!
NERGAL, God of the Sacrifice of Blood, Remember!
NERGAL, Lord of the Offerings of Battle, Ravager of the Enemy's Towns,
Devourer of the flesh of Man, Remember!
NERGAL, Wielder of the Mighty Sword, Remember!
NERGAL, Lord of Arms and Armies, Remember!

Spirit of the Glow of the Battlefield, Open wide Thy Gate! Spirit of
the Entrance Unto Death, Open Thy Gate to me!

Spirit of the Sailing Lance, the Thrusting Sword, the Flying Rock, Open
the Gate to Thy Sphere to One who has no fear!

Gate of the Red Planet, Open!
Gate of the God of War, Swing Wide!
Gate of the God of Victory got in Battle, Open to me! Gate
of the Lord of Protection, Open!
Gate of the Lord of the ARRA and the AGGA, Open!
By the Name which I was given on the Sphere of SHAMMASH, I ask Thee, Open! IA
NERGAL-YA! IA ZI ANNGA KANPA!
IA NNGA! IA NNGR-YA! IA! NNGYA! IA ZI DINGIR NEENYA KANPA! IA
KANTALAMAKKYA TARRA! KANPA!

THE INVOCATION OF THE MARDUK GATE

Spirit of the Great Planet, Remember!

MARDUK, God of Victory Over the Dark Angels, Remember!
MARDUK, Lord of All the Lands, Remember!
MARDUK, Son of ENKI, Master of Magicians, Remember! MARDUK,
Vanquisher of the Ancient Ones, Remember! MARDUK, Who gives the
Stars their Powers, Remember! MARDUK, Who assigns the Wanderers
their Places, Remember! Lord of the Worlds, and of The Spaces Between,
Remember! First among the Astral Gods, Hearken and Remember!

In the Name of the Covenant sworn between Thee and the Race of Men I call
to Thee! Hearken and Remember!
From the Gate of the Mighty NERGAL, the Sphere of the Red Planet, I call
to Thee! Hearken and Remember!
MARDUK, Lord of the Fifty Powers, Open Thy Gates to me! MARDUK,
God of Fifty Names, Open Thy Gates to Thy Servant!

By the Name which I was given on the Sphere of NERGAL, I call to Thee to Open!

Gate of the Great God, Open!

Gate of the God of the Double-Headed Axe, Open!
Gate of the Lord of the World Between the Worlds, Open! Gate
of the Conqueror of the Monsters from the Sea, Open! Gate of the
Golden City of SAGALLA, Open!
IA DAG! IA GAT! IA MARGOLQBABBONNESH!
IA MARRUTUKKU! IA TUKU! SUHRIM SUHGURIM!
ZAHRIM ZAHGURIM! AXXANNGABANNAXAXAGANNABABILLUKUKU!

THE INVOCATION OF THE NINIB GATE

Spirit of the Wanderer of the Wastes, Remember! Spirit of
the Planet of Time, Remember!

Spirit of the Plane of he Hunter, Remember! NINIB,
Lord of the Dark Ways, Remember! NINIB, Lord of the
Secret Passages, Remember!

NINIB, Knower of the Secrets of All Things, Remember! NINIB,
Knower of the Ways of the Ancient Ones, Remember! NINIB,
Horned One of Silence, Remember!
NINIB, Watcher of the Ways of the IGIGI, Remember! NINIB,
Knower of the Pathways of the Dead, Remember!

In the Name of the Covenant sworn between Thee and the Race of Men, I call
to Thee! Hearken and Remember!
From the Mighty Gate of the Lord of Gods, MARDUK, Sphere of the Great Planet, I call
to Thee! Hearken and Remember!

NINIB, Dark Wandered of the Forgotten Lands, Hearken and Remember! NINIB,
Gatekeeper of the Astral Gods, Open Thy Gate to me!

NINIB, Master of the Chase and the Long Journey, Open Thy Gate to me! Gate
of the Double-Horned Elder God, Open!
Gate of the Last City of the Skies, Open! Gate of
the Secret of All Time, Open!

Gate of the Master of Magickal Power, Open! Gate of
the Lord of All Sorcery, Open!

Gate of the Vanquisher of all Evil Spells, Hearken and Open!
By the Name which I was given on the Sphere of MARDUK, Master of Magicians, I call
Thee to Open!
IA DUK! IA ANDARRA! IA ZI BATTU BA ALLU!
BALLAGU BEL DIRRIGU BAAGGA KA KANPA! BEL
ZI EXA EXA!
AZZAGBAT! BAZZAGBARRONIOSH!
ZELIG!

THE CONJURATION OF THE FIRE GOD

Spirit of the Fire, Remember! GIBIL,
Spirit of the Fire, Remember!

GIRRA, Spirit of the Flames, Remember!
O God of Fire, Mighty Son of ANU, Most terrifying among Thy Brothers, Rise!
O God of the Furnace, God of Destruction, Remember!
Rise Up, O God of Fire, GIBIL in Thy Majesty, and devour my enemies!
Rise up, O God of Fire, GIRRA in Thy Power, and burn the sorcerers who
persecute me!
GIBIL GASHRU UMANA YANDURU
TUSHTE YESH SHIR ILLANI U MA YALKI!
GISHBAR IA ZI IA
IA ZI DINGIR GIRRA KANPA!
Rise up, Son of the Flaming Disk of ANU!
Rise up, Offspring of the Golden Weapon of MARDUK!
It is not I , but ENKI, Master of the Magicians, who summons Thee!
It is not I, but MARDUK, Slayer of the Serpent, who calls Thee here now!
Burn the Evil and the Evildoer!
Burn the Sorcerer and the Sorceress!
Singe them! Burn them! Destroy them!
Consume their powers!
Carry them away!
Rise up, GISHBAR BA GIBBIL BA GIRRA ZI AGA KANPA!
Spirit of the God of Fire, Thou art Conjured!
KAKKAMMANUNU!

THE CONJURATION OF THE WATCHER

THIS is the Book of the Conjuration of the Watcher, for formulae as I received them from the
Scribe of ENKI, Our Master and Lord of All Magick. Great care must be taken that this
untamed Spirit does not rise up against the Priest, and for that reason a preliminary sacrifice
must be made in a clean and new bowl with the appropriate sigils inscribed thereupon, being
the three grey carven signs of the Rock of my initiation, which

are:

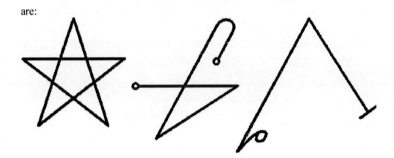

They must be engraved upon the bowl with a fine stylus, or painted thereon with dark ink. The sacrifice must be new bread, pine resin, and the grass Olieribos. These must be burned in the new bowl, and the Sword of the Watcher, with his Sigil engraved thereupon, at hand, for he will inhabit such at the time of the Calling of the Watcher and will depart when he is given license to depart.

The Watcher comes from a Race different from that of Men and yet different from that of the Gods, and it is said that he was with KINGU and his hordes at the time of the War between the Worlds, but was dissatisfied and did cleave unto the Armies of Lord MARDUK.

Wherefore it is wise to conjure It in the Names of the Three Great Watchers Who existed before the Confrontation from whose borne the Watcher and His Race ultimately derive, and those Three are ANU, ENLIL, and Master ENKI of the Magick Waters. And for this reason They are sometimes called the Three Watchers, MASS SSARATI and the Watcher MASS SSARATU, or KIA MASS SSARATU.

And the Watcher appears sometimes as a great and fierce Dog, who prowls about the Gate or the Circle, frightening away the idimmu who forever lurk about the barriers, waiting for sacrifice. And the Watcher aloft the Sword of Flames, and even the Elder Gods are awed thereby. And sometimes the Watcher appears as a Man in A long Robe, shaven, with eyes that never lose their stare. And the Lord of the Watchers dwells, it is said, among the Wastes of the IGIGI, and only Watches and never raises the Sword or fights the idimmi, save when the Covenant is invoked by none less than the Elder Gods in their Council, like unto the Seven Glorious APHKHALLU.

And sometimes the Watcher appears as the Enemy, ready to devour the Priest who has erred in the incantations, or omitted the sacrifice, or acted in defiance of the Covenant, for which acts the very Elder Gods cannot forbid that silent Race from exacting its toll. And it is said that some of that Race lie waiting for the Ancient Ones to once more rule

the Cosmos, that they may be given the right hand of honour, and that such as these are lawless. This is what is said.

THE PRELIMINARY INVOCATION

When the time has come to summon the Watcher the first time, the place of thy calling must be clean, and a double circle of flour drawn about thee. And there should be no altar, but only the new Bowl with the three carven signs on it. And the Conjuration of the Fire should be made, and the sacrifices heaped thereupon, into the burning bowl. And the Bowl is now called AGA MASS SSARATU, and to be used for no other purpose, save to invoke the Watcher.

And the bowl must be lain between the Circles, facing the Northeast.
And thy vestments should be black, and thy cap black.

And the Sword must be at hand, but not yet in the ground.
And it must be the Darkest Hour of the Night.
And there must be no light, save for the AGA MASS SSARATU.
And the Conjuration of the Three must be made, thus:

ISS MASS SSARATI SHA MUSHI LIPSHURU RUXISHA
LIMNUTI! IZIZANIMMA ILANI RABUTI SHIMA YA DABABI!

DINA DINA ALAKTI LIMDA!
ALSI KU NUSHI ILANI MUSHITI!

IA MASS SSARATI ISS MASS SSARATI BA IDS MASS SSARATU!

And this special Conjuration may be made at any time the Priest feels he is in danger, whether his life or his spirit, and the Three Watchers and the One Watcher will rush to his aid.

This being said, at the words IDS MASS SSARATU the Sword must be thrust into the ground behind the AGA MASS SSARATU with force. And the Watcher will appear for the instructions to be made by the Priest.

THE NORMAL INVOCATION OF THE WATCHER

This Invocation is to be made during the course of any Ceremony when it is necessary to summon the Watcher to preside over the outer precincts of the Circle or Gate. The Sword is to be thrust into the ground as before, in the Northeast section, but the AGA MASS SSARATU is not necessary LEST THOU HAST NOT MADE SACRIFICE TO THINE WATCHER IN THE SPACE OF ONE MOON in which case it is necessary to sacrifice to It anew whether in that Ceremony or at some other, earlier.

Raise the Copper Dagger of INANNA of the Calling, and declaim the Invocation in a clear voice, be it loud or soft:

IA MASS SSARATU!

I conjure Thee by the Fire of GIRRA
The Veils of Sunken Varloorni, And by
the Lights of SHAMMASH.

I call Thee here, before me, in visible shadow
In beholdable Form, to Watch and Protect this Sacred Circle, this Holy Gate of (N.)
May He of the Name Unspeakable, the Number Unknowable,
Whom no man hath seen at any time,
Whom no geometer measureth,
Whom no wizard hath ever called
CALL THEE HERE NOW!
Rise up, by ANU I summon Thee! Rise
up, by ENLIL I summon Thee! Rise up,
by ENKI I summon Thee! Cease to be
the Sleeper of EGURRA.

Cease to lie unwaking beneath the Mountains of KUR.
Rise up, from the pits of ancient holocausts!

Rise up, from the old Abyss of NARR MARRATU!
Come, by ANU!
Come, by ENLIL!
Come, by ENKI!

In the Name of the Covenant, Come and Rise up before me!

IA MASS SSARATU! IA MASS SSARATU! IA MASS SSARATU ZI KIA KANPA!
BARRGOLOMOLONETH KIA!

SHTAH!

At this point, the Watcher will surely come and stand outside the Gate or Circle until such
time as he is given the license to depart by striking of the Priest's left hand on the hilt of the
Sword, while pronouncing the formula BARRA MASS SSARATU! BARRA!

Thou mayest not depart thine sacred precincts until the Watcher has been given this
license, else he will devour thee. Such are the laws.

And he care not what he Watches, only that he obey the Priest.

THE BOOK MAKLU OF THE BURNING OF EVIL

SPIRITS

HERE are the Banishments, the Burnings, and the Bindings handed down to us by ENKI,
the Master. They are to be performed over the AGA MASS SSARATU by the Priest,
with the appropriate images as described herein. The incantations must be recited after
the Watcher has been summoned, and he will do the deeds set down for him by the
incantations. When he returns, he is to be dismissed as set down previously. Know that,
when images are used, they must be burned utterly, and the ashes buried in safe ground
where none may find them, else to touch them would mean death.

Know that the Evil Spirits are principally Seven, for the Seven Maskim who tear away
the heart of a man and mock his Gods. And their Magick is very strong, and they are the
Lords over the shadows and over the depths of the Seas, and reigned once, it is said, over
MAGAN, whence they came. The banishings, or exorcisms, are to be pronounced in a
clear voice without trembling, without shaking. The arms should be held over the head in
the attitude of a Priest of SHAMMASH, and the eyes must behold the Spirit of the God
SHAMMASH, even though it be the time of the Sleeping of SHAMMASH behind the
Mountains of the Scorpion.

No word must be changed. These must not be shown to any but the properly instructed. To show them to anyone Other is to ask the curse of NINNGHIZHIDA on yourself and upon your generations.

The Book MAKLU of the Burnings:

THE EXORCISM OF THE CROWN OF ANU

The Priest, in time of peril, shall put on the spotless white crown of ANU with the Eight-rayed Seal and stand in the prescribed manner with the Tablets of Calling on his breast and the copper Dagger of INANNA in his right hand, aloft.

For, it is said, if a man builds a fire, does he no build it in a Pit, that he might not be harmed thereby? Thus is it true of the UDUGGU we call, for they are like Fire and every caution must be used lest they consume the magician and his entire generation.

Thus, the Exorcism of ANU

I have put the Starry Crown of Heaven, the potent Disk of ANU on my head
That a kindly Spirit and a kindly Watcher

Like the God that hath made me
May stand at my head always

To life me to favour with the Elder Gods

UDUGGHUL

ALLACHUL
MALLACHUL
MASQIMCHUL
DINGIRCHUL
No Evil Spirit
No Evil Demon
No Evil God
No Evil Fiend
No Hag Demon
No Filth-Eating Demon
No Thieving Demon
No Shadow of the Night
No Shell of the Night
No Mistress of the Demon

No Offspring of the Demon
No Evil Spell
No Enchantment
No Sorcery
NO EVIL IN THE WORLD OR UNDER IT
OVER THE WORLD OR INSIDE THE WORLD
MAY SEIZE ME HERE!
BARRA ANTE MALDA!
BARRA ANGE GE YENE!
ZI DINGIR ANNA KANPA!
ZI DINGIR KIA KANPA!
GAGGAMANNU!

A CONJURATION AGAINST THE SEVEN LIERS-IN-WAIT

They are Seven They are Seven

In the depths of the ocean, they are Seven In the shining
heavens, they are Seven They proceed from the ocean
depths They proceed from the hidden retreat They are
neither male nor female
These which stretch themselves out like chains They have no
spouse
They beget not children They are strangers to
charity They ignore prayers
They scoff at wishes
They are vermin that come forth from the Mountains of MASHU

Enemies of Our Master ENKI

They are the vengeance of the Ancient Ones
Raising up difficulties
Obtaining power through wickedness
The Enemies! The Enemies! The Seven Enemies!
They are Seven!
They are Seven!
They are Seven times Seven!
Spirit of the Sky, Remember! Spirit of the Earth, Remember!

THE EXORCISM BARRA EDINNAZU FOR SPIRITS WHO ATTACK THE CIRCLE

ZI ANNA KANPA!

ZI KIA KANPA!
GALLU BARRA!
NAMTAR BARRA!
ASHAK BARRA!
GIGIM BARRA!
ALAL BARRA!
TELAL BARRA!
MASQIM BARRA!
UTUQ BARRA!
IDPA BARRA!
LALARTU BARRA!
LALLASSU BARRA!
AKHKHARU BARRA!
URUKKU BARRA!
KIELGALAL BARRA!
LILITU BARRA!
UTUQ XUL EDIN NA ZU!
ALLA XUL EDIN NA ZU!
GIGIM XUL EDIN NA ZU!
MULLA XUL EDIN NA ZU!
DINGIRXUL EDIN NA ZU!
MASQIM XUL EDIN NA ZU!
BARRA!
EDINNAZU!
ZI ANNA KANPA! ZI KIA KANPA!

THE EXORCISM ZI DINGIR

(To be used against any kind of malefick)

ZI DINGIR NNGI E NE KANPA

ZI DINGIR NINGI E NE KANPA
ZI DINGIR ENNUL E NE KANPA
ZI DINGIR NINNUL E NE KANPA
ZI DINGIR ENN KURKUR E NE KANPA
ZI DINGIR NINN KURKUR E NE KANPA
ZI DINGIR N DA SHURRIM MA KANPA

ZI DINGIR NINNDA SHURRIM MA KANPA ZI
DINGIR ENDUL AAZAG GA KANPA

ZI DINGIR NINNDUL AAZAG GA KANPA ZI
DINGIR ENUHDDIL LA KANPA

ZI DINGIR NINN UHDDIL LA KANPA
ZI DINGIR ENMESHIR RAA KANPA ZI
DINGIR NINNME SHIR RAA KANPA
ZI DINGIR ENAA MAA A DINGIR ENLIL LAAGE KANPA
ZI DINGIR NINNA MAA A DINGIR NINNLIL LAAGE KANPA
ZI DINGIR SSISGI GISH MA SAGBA DAA NI IDDA ENNUBALLEMA KANPA ZI
DINGIR BHABBHAR L'GAL DEKUD DINGIR RI ENNEGE KANPA

ZI DINGIR NINNI DUGGAANI DINGIR A NNUNNA IA AN SAGGNNUUNGA
GATHA GAN ENE KANPA!

THE EXORCISM AGAINST AZAG-THOTH AND HIS EMISSARIES

(An image must be made of a throne-chair, and put into the flames of the AGA MASS SSARATU while chanting the following exorcism.)

Boil! Boil! Burn! Burn!

UTUK XUL TA ARDATA!
Who art thou, whose son?
Who are thou, whose daughter?
What sorcery, what spells, has brought thee here?
May ENKI, the Master of Magicians, free me!
May ASHARILUDU, son of ENKI, free me!
May they bring to nought your vile sorceries!
I chain you!
I bind you!
I deliver you to GIRRA
Lord of the Flames
Who sears, burns, enchains
Of whom even mighty KUTULU has fear!
May GIRRA, the Ever-burning One gives strenght to my arms!

May GIBIL, the Lord of Fire, givepower to my Magick!
Injustice, murder, freezing of the loins,

Rending of the bowels, devouring of the flesh, and madness In all
ways hast thou persecuted me!
Mad God of CHAOS! May
GIRRA free me!

AZAG-THOTH TA ARDATA! IA MARDUK! IA MARDUK! IA ASALLUXI! You
have chosen me for a corpse.
You have delivered me to the Skull. You
have sent Phantoms to haunt me. You have
send vampires to haunt me.
To the wandering Ghosts of the Wastes, have you delivered me. To the
Phantoms of the fallen ruins, have you delivered me.

To the deserts, the wastes, the forbidden lands, you have handed me over. Open
Thy Mouth In Sorceries Against Me No More!
I have handed thine image over Into
the flames of GIBIL! Burn, Mad
Fiend!
Boil, Mad God!
May the Burning GIRRA untie thy knots! May the
Flames of GIBIL untie your cord! May the Law of the
Burning seize your throat! May the Law of the Burning
avenge me!

It is not I, but MARDUK, son of ENKI, Masters in Magick, that commands Thee!

KAKKAMMU! KANPA!

INCANTATION AGAINST THE ANCIENT ONES

(To be recited each year, when the Bear hangs from its Tail in the Heavens)

Destructive Storms and Evil Winds are they

An evil blast, herald of the baneful storm
An evil blast, forerunner of the baneful storm
They are mighty children, Ancient Ones
Heralds of Pestilence
Throne-bearers of NINNKIGAL
They are the flood which rusheth through the Land

Seven Gods of the Broad Heavens

Seven Gods of the Broad Earth
Seven Ancient Ones are They
Seven Gods of Might

Seven Evil Gods

Seven Evil Demons
Seven Demons of Oppression
Seven in Heaven
Seven on Earth

UTUG XUL

ALA XUL
GIDIM XUL
MULLA XUL
DINGIR XUL
MASQIM XUL
ZI ANNA KANPA!
ZI KIA KANPA
ZI DINGIR ENLIL LA LUGAL KURKUR RA GE KANPA!
ZI DINGIR NINLIL LA NIN KURKUR RA GE KANPA!
ZI DINGIR NINIB IBILA ESHARRA GE KANPA!
ZI DINGIR NINNI NIN KURKUR RA GE KANPA!
ZI DINGIR A NUNNA DINGIR GALGALLA E NE KANPA!
ZI DINGIR ANNA KANPA!
ZI DINGIR KIA KANPA!

BABABARARARA ANTE MALDADA!

BABABARARARA ANTE GEGE ENENE!

INCANTATION OF PROTECTION AGAINST THE WORKERS OF THE
ANCIENT ONES

SHAMMASH SHA KASHSHAPIYA KASSHAP TIYA

EPISHYA MUSHTEPISH TIYA!
Kima Tinur khuturshuna l'rim!
Lichulu Lizubu u Littaattuku!
E Pishtashunu Kima meh naadu ina tikhi likhtu!

SHUNU LIMUTUMA ANAKU LU'UBLUYI!

SHUNU LINISHUMA ANAKU LU'UDNIN!
SHUNU LI'IKTISHUMA ANAKU LUUPPATARI!
Tirrama shaluti Sha Kashshapti Sha Ruchi ye
Ipushu
Shupi yi arkhish Uppu yush!
ZI DINGIR GAL KESHSHEBA KANPA!

(This to be recited Seven times in the Circle of Flour before the AGA MASS SSARATU when it is found that the worshippers of TIAMAT are raising Powers against thee or thy

neighbourhood. Or, it may said when the Great Bear is suspended from his Tail in the Heavens, which is the Time the baneful worshippers gather for their Rites, and by which they mark their calendar. The mercy of ANU be upon thee!)

THE EXORCISM AGAINST THE POSSESSING SPIRIT

(This to be said when the body of possessed is distant, or when secrecy must be maintained. To be performed within thy Circle, before the Watcher.)

The wicked God

The wicked Demon
The Demon of the Desert
The Demon of the Mountain
The Demon of the Sea
The Demon of the Marsh
The wicked Genius
The Enormous Larvae
The wicked Winds
The Demon that seizeth the body
The Demon that rendeth the body
SPIRIT OF THE SKY, REMEMBER!
SPIRIT OF THE EARTH, REMEMBER!

The Demon that seizeth man

The Demon that seizeth man
The GIGIM who worketh Evil
The Spawn of the wicked Demon
SPIRIT OF THE SKY, REMEMBER!
SPIRIT OF THE EARTH, REMEMBER!

He who forges images

He who casts spells
The Evil Angel
The Evil Eye
The Evil Mouth
The Evil Tongue
The Evil Lip
The Most Perfect Sorcery
SPIRIT OF THE SKY, REMEMBER!
SPIRIT OF THE EARTH, REMEMBER!

NINNKIGAL, Spouse of NINNAZU

May she cause him to turn his face toward the Place where she is!
May the wicked Demons depart!

May they seize one another!

May they feed on one another's bones!
SPIRIT OF THE SKY, REMEMBER!
SPIRIT OF THE EARTH, REMEMBER!

THE EXORCISM ANNAKIA

(A conjuration of Heaven and Earth and All Between against the Possessing Spirit, to be recited seven times over the body of the possessed person till the spirit issueth forth from his nose and mouth in the form of liquid and fire, like unto green oils. Then the person shall be whole, and shall sacrifice to INANNA at her Temple. And this must not be omitted, lest the spirit return to what INANNA has cast off.)

ZI DINGIR ANNA KANPA!
ZI DINGIR KIA KANPA! ZI
DINGIR URUKI KANPA! ZI
DINGIR NEBO KANPA!

ZI DINGIR ISHTAR KANPA!
ZI DINGIR SHAMMASH UDDU KANPA!
ZI DINGIR NERGAL KANPA!
ZI DINGIR MARDUK KANPA!
ZI DINGIR NINIB ADDAR KANPA!
ZI DINGIR IGIGI KANPA!
ZI DINGIR ANNUNNAKIA KANPA

ZI DINGIR ENLIL LA LUGAL KURKURRAGE KANPA! ZI
DINGIR NENLIL LA NINKURKURRAGE KANPA! ZI
DINGIR NINIB IBBILA ESHARRAGE KANPA!

ZI DINGIR NINNINI KURKURRAGE GIGSHI INN BHABBHARAGE KANPA!
ZI DINGIR ANNUNNA DINGIR GALGALLAENEGE KANPA!
KAKAMMU!

THE BINDING OF THE EVIL SORCERERS

*(When thou art haunted by the spells of the worshippers of the Ancient Ones, make
images of them, one male and one female, and burn them in the flames of the AGA MASS
SSARATU, while pronouncing the following Incantation of the Binding:)*

I invoke you, Gods of the Night

Together with you I call to the Night, to the Covered Woman
I call in the Evening, at Midnight, and in the Morning
Because they have enchanted me
The sorcerer and the sorceress have bound me

My God and my Goddess cry over me.

I am plagued with pain because of illness. I
stand upright, I cannot lie down
Neither during the night nor during the day.
They have stuffed my mouth with cords! They
have closes my mouth with grass!

They have made the water of my drink scarce.
My joy is sorrow, and my merriment is grief.
Arise! Great Gods! Hear my waiting!   .
Obtain justice! Take notice of my Ways!
I have an image of the sorcerer and the sorceress,
Of my enchanter and enchantress.
May the Three Watches of the Night dissolve their evil sorceries!
May their mouths be wax, their tongues honey.
The word of my doom which they have spoken,
May they melt like wax!
The spell that they worked, may it pour away like honey.
Their knot it broken!
Their work destroyed!

All their speech fills the deserts and the wastes
According to the Decree which the Gods of the Night have issued. It
is finished.

ANOTHER BINDING OF THE SORCERERS

(Take a cord with ten knots. As you recite each line of the incantation, untie one knot.
When this is finished, throw the cord into the flames and give thanks to the Gods)

My images have you given over to the dead; turn back! My
images have you seen with the dead; turn back!

My images have you thrown to the side of the dead; turn back! My
images have you thrown to the ground of the dead; turn back! My
images have you buried in the coffin with the dead; turn back! My
images have you given over to the destruction; turn back! My
images have you enclosed with walls; turn back!
My images have you struck down on doorsteps; turn back! My
images have you locked into the gate of wall; turn back! My
images have you given over to the God of Fire; turn back!

A MOST EXCELLENT CHARM AGAINST THE HORDES OF DEMONS
THAT ASSAIL IN THE NIGHT

(May be chanted while walking around the circumference of the Circle, and sprinkling
the vicinity with sweet water, using a pine cone or golden brush. An image of a Fish may
be at hand, and the incantation pronounced clearly, every word, either whispered softly,
or shouted loudly.)

ISA YA! ISA YA! RI EGA! RI EGA!

BI ESHA BI ESHA! XIYILQA! XIYILQA!
DUPPIRA ATLAKA ISA YA U RI EGA
LIMUTTIKUNU KIMA QUTRI LITILLI SHAMI YE
INA ZUMRI YA ISA YA
INA ZUMRI YA RI EGA
INA ZUMRI YA BI ESHA
INA ZUMRI YA XIYILQA
INA ZUMRI YA DUPPIRA
INA ZUMRI YA ATLAKA

INA ZUMRI YA LA TATARA
INA ZUMRI YA LA TETIXXI YE
INA ZUMRI YA LA TAQARRUBA
INA ZUMRI YA LA TASANIQA
NI YISH SHAMMASH KABTU LU TAMATUNU
NI YISH ENKI BEL GIMRI LU TAMATUNU
NI YISH MARDUK MASHMASH ILANI LU TAMATUNU
NI YISH GISHBAR QAMIKUNU LU TAMATUNU
INA ZUMRI YA LU YU TAPPARRASAMA!

THE CONJURATION OF THE MOUNTAINS OF MASHU

(A spell to cause consternation in the Enemy, and confuse his thoughts. It is also a binding, that the evil sorcerer may not see his spells work their desired ends, but melt away like honey or wax. These Mountains are called SHADU, and are the hiding places of the Serpents of KUR. A spell to cause ultimate destruction.)

SHADU YU LIKTUMKUNUSHI

SHADU YU LIKLAKUNUSHI
SHADU YU LINI YIX KUNUSHI
SHADU YU LI YIXSI KUNUSHI
SHADU YU LITE KUNUSHI
SHADU YU LINI KUNUSHI
SHADU YU LINIR KUNUSHI
SHADU YU LIKATTIN KUNUSHI
SHADU YU DANNU ELIKUNU LIMQUT
INA ZUMRI YA LU YU TAPPARRASAMA!

THE BOOK OF CALLING

THIS is the Book of the Ceremonies of Calling, handed down since the time the Elder Gods walked the Earth, Conquerors of the Ancient Ones.

This is the Book of NINNGHIZHIDDA, Horned Serpent, the Lady of the Magick Wand.
This is the Book of NINAXAKUDDU, The Queen, Mistress of the Incantations.

This is the Book of ASALLUXI, the King, the Lord of Magick.
This is the Book of AZAG, the Enchanter.
This is the Book of EGURA, the Dark Waters of ABSU, Realm of ERESHKIGAL, Queen of Death.
This is the Book of the Ministers of Knowledge, FIRIK and PIRIK, the Demon of the Snake-Entwined Magick Wand and the Demon of the Thunderbolt, Protectors of the Arcane Faith, the Most Secret Knowledge, to be hidden from those not of us, from the uninitiated.
This is the Book of ASARU, the Eye on the Throne.
This is the book of USHUMGALLUM, Mighty Dragon, born of HUBUR, of the Battle Against the Elder Gods.
This is the Book of ENDUKUGGA and NINDUKUGGA, Male and Female Monsters of the Abyss, of the Claws like Daggers and the Wings of Darkness.
This is further the Book of NAMMTAR, Chief among the Magicians of ERESHKIGAL.
This is the Book of the Seven Demons of the Ignited Spheres, of the Seven Demons of the Flame.
This is the Book of the Priest, who governeth the Works of Fire!

Know, first, that the Power of the Conquerors is the Power of the Magick, and that the stricken gods will ever tempt thee away from the Legions of the Mighty, and that you will feel the subtle fluids of thy body moving to the breath of TIAMAT and the Blood of KINGU who races in your veins. Be ever watchful, therefore, not to open this Gate, or, if thou must needs, put a time for its closing before the rising of the Sun, and seal it at that time; for to leave it open is to be the agent of CHAOS.

Know, secondly, that the Power of Magick is the Power of Our Master ENKI, Lord of the Seas, and Master of Magick, Father of MARDUK, Fashioner of the Magick Name, the Magick Number, the Magick Word, the Magick Shape. So, therefore, the Priest who governeth the works of Fire, and of the God of Fire, GISHBAR called GIBIL, must firstly sprinkle with the Water of the Seas of ENKI, as a testament to his Lordship and a sign of the Covenant that exists between him and thee.

Know, thirdly, that by the Power of the Elder Gods and the submission of the Ancient

Ones, thou mayest procure every type of honour, dignity, wealth and happiness, but that these are to be shunned as the Purveyors of Death, for the most radiant jewels are to be found buried deep in the Earth, and the Tomb of Man is the Splendour of ERESHKIGAL, the joy of KUTULU, the food of AZAG-THOTH.

Therefore, thine obligation is as of the Gatekeep of the Inside, agent of MARDUK, servant of ENKI, for the Gods are forgetful, and very far away, and it was to the Priests of the Flame that Covenant was given to seal the Gates between this World and the

Other, and to keep Watch thereby, through this Night of Time, and the Circle of Magick is the Barrier, the Temple, and the Gate between the Worlds.

Know, fourthly, that it is become the obligation of the Priests of the Flame and the Sword, and of all Magick, to bring their Power to the Underworld and keep it chained thereby, for the Underworld is surely the Gate Forgotten, by which the Ancient Ones ever seek Entrance to the Land of the Living, And the Ministers of ABSU are clearly walking the Earth, riding on the Air, and upon the Earth, and sailing silently through the Water, and roaring in the Fire, and all these Spirits must be brought to subjection to the Person of the Priest of Magick, before any else. Or the Priest becomes prey to the Eye of Death of the Seven ANNUNNAKI, Lord of the Underworld, Ministers of the Queen of Hell.

Know, fifthly, that the worshippers of TIAMAT are abroad in the world, and will give fight to the Magician. Lo, they have worshipped the Serpent from Ancient Times, and have always been with us. And they are to be known by their seeming human appearance which has the mark of the Beast upon them, as they change easily into the Shapes of animals and haunt the Nights of Men and by their odour, which comes of burning incenses unlawful to the worship of the Elder Ones. And their Books are the Books of CHAOS and the flames, and are the Books of the Shadows and the Shells. And they worship the heaving earth and the ripping sky and the rampant flame and the flooding waters; and they are the raisers of the legions of maskim, the Liers-In-Wait. And they do not know what it is they do, but they do it at the demands of the Serpent, at whose Name even ERESHKIGAL gives fright, and the dread KUTULU strains at his bonds:

MUMMU TIAMAT Queen of the Ancient Ones!

Know, sixthly, that thou shalt not seek the operations of this Magick save by the rules and governments set down herein, for to do other is to take the most awful risk, for thyself and for all mankind. Therefore, heed these words carefully, and change not the words of the incantations, whether thou understand them, or understand them not, for they are the words of the Pacts made of Old, and before Time. So, say them softly if the formula is "softly", or shout them aloud if the formula is "aloud", but change not one measure lest thou call something Else, and it be your final hour.

Know, seventhly, of the Things thou art to expect in the commission of this Most sacred Magick. Study the symbols well, and do not be afraid of any awful spectre that shall

invade thine operation, or haunt thine habitat by day or by night. Only charge them with them the words of the Covenant and they will do as you ask, of thou be strong. And if thou performest these operations often, thou shalt see things becoming dark; and the Wanderers in their Spheres shall no more be seen by thee; and the Stars in their places will lose their Light, and the Moon, NANNA, by whom thou also workest, shall become black and extinguished,

AND ARATAGAR SHALL BE NO MORE, AND THE EARTH SHALL ABIDE NOT

And around thee shall appear the Flame, like Lightning flashing in all directions, and all things will appear amid thunders, and from the Cavities of the Earth will leap forth the ANNUNNAKI, Dog-Faced, and thou shalt bring them down.

And the Sign of your Race is this:

Which thou shalt wear at all times, as the Sign of the Covenant between thee and the Elder Gods. And the Sign of the Elder Ones is this:

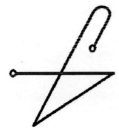

Which thou shalt wear at all times, as the sign of the Power of the Magick of ENKI. And I have told thee all this before, but I tell thee again, for the Priest, being furnished with every kind of Armour, and armed, he is similar to the Goddess.

The Place of Calling shall be high in the Mountains, most preferably; or near the Sea; or in some secluded area far from the thoughts of Man; or in the desert; or atop an ancient temple. And it shall be clean, and free from the unwanted. Thus, the Place, once chosen, shall be purified by supplications to thine particular God and Goddess, and by burning offerings of pine and cedar. And a round load shall be brought, and salt. And, having offered it to the personal deities, the Priest shall pronounce, solemnly, the following exorcism that the Place of Calling be cleansed and all Evil that the Place of Calling be cleansed and all Evil banished thereby; and the Priest shall not change one word or letter of this exorcism, but recite it faithfully as it is put down:

ENU SHUB

AM GIG ABSU
KISH EGIGGA
GAR SHAG DA SISIE AMARDA YA
DINGIR UD KALAMA SINIKU
DINGIR NINAB GUYU NEXRRANIKU

GA YA SHU SHAGMUKU TU!

And they Bread burned in the bronze brazier of Calling: and the Salt scattered about the room, sixty times.

And a Circle shall be drawn on the ground, in the midst whereof you shall stand while reciting the conjurations set forth, taking especial care not to venture forth from the boundaries of the Circle, the holy MANDAL of Calling, lest thou be consumed by the invisible monsters from the EGURRA of ERESHKIGAL, as was the Priest ABDUL BEN-MARTU in a public square in Jerusalem.

And the Circle shall be drawn in lime, or barley, or white flour. Or dug in the ground with the Dagger of INANNA of Calling. Or embroidered in the most precious silk, or expensive cloth.

And the colours thereof shall be only black and white, and no other.

And the Frontlet of Calling, and the Standards of Calling, shall all be of fine cloth, and in the colours of NINIB and INANNA, that is, of Black and White, for NINIB knows the Outer Regions and the ways of the Ancient Ones, and INANNA subdued the Underworld and vanquished the Queen thereof

And the Crown of Calling shall bear the Eight-Rayed Star of the Elder Gods, and may be of beaten copper, set in with precious stones.

And thou shalt bear with thee a Rod of lapis lazuli, the Five-Rayed Star about thy neck, the Frontlet, the Girdle, the Amulet of UR about thine Arm, and a pure and unspotted Robe.

And these things shall be worn for the Operations of Calling only, and at other times shall be put away and hid, so that no eye may see them, save your own. As for the worship of the Gods, it is after the fashion of your country, but the Priests of Old were naked in their rites.

And thou shalt put down the Circle. And thou shalt invoke thy God and thy Goddess, but their Images must be removed from the altar and put away, unless thou call the Powers of MARDUK, in which case an Image of MARDUK should be set thereupon, and no other. And the perfumes must be burnt in the brazier this Book. And the Watcher summoned, after Its fashion. And the Four Gates invoked, being the Four Watchtowers that stand about thee and the circumference of the MANDAL and witness the Rites, and Watch the Outside, that the Ancient Ones may not trouble thee.

And the Invocations of the Four Gates is after this fashion, which thou recite loudly, in a clear voice:

OF THE INVOCATION OF THE FOUR GATES FROM THE WORLD BETWEEN THE SPHERES

Invocation of the North Gate

Thee I invoke, Silver Hunter from the Sacred City of UR!

Thee I call forth to guard this North Place of the Most Holy Mandal against the vicious warriors of Flame from the Principalities of DRA!
Be thou most vigilant against the UTUKKI of TIAMAT
The Oppressors of ISHNIGARRAB
The Throne of AZAG-THOTH!
Draw Thy bow before the fiends of ABSU
Loose Thy arrow at the hordes of Dark Angels that beset the beloved of ARRA on all sides and in all places.

Be watchful, Lord of the North Ways.
Remember us, King of our Homeland, Victor of Every War and Conqueror over Every Adversary.
See our Lights and hear our Heralds, and do not forsake us.
Spirit of the North, Remember!

Invocation of the Eastern Gate

Thee I invoke, Mistress of the Rising Star. Queen
of Magick, of the Mountains of MASHU!

Thee I call forth this day to guard this Most Holy mandal against the Seven Ensnarers, the Seven Liers-In-Wait, the evil Maskim, the Evil Lords!

Thee I Summon, Queen of the Eastern Ways, that thou mayest protect me from the Eye of Death, and the evil rays of the ENDUKUGGA and NINDUKUGGA!

Be watchful, Queen of the Eastern Ways, and Remember!
Spirit of the East, Remember!

Invocation of the Southern Gate

Thee I invoke, Angel, Guardian against the URULU Dread City of Death, Gate of No Return!

Do Thou stand at my side!
In the Names of the most Mighty Hosts of MARDUK and ENKI, Lords of the Elder Race, the ARRA, do Thou stand firm behind me!
Against PAZUZU and HUMWAVA, Fiends of the Southwest Winds, do Thou stand form!
Against the Lords of the Abominations, do Thou stand form!
Be Thou the Eyes behind me,
The Sword behind me,
The Spear behind me,
The Armour behind me.
Be watchful, Spirit of the Southern Ways, and Remember!
Spirit of the South, Remember!

The Invocation of the Western Gate

Thee I invoke, Spirit of the Land of MER MARTU!
Thee I invoke, Angel of the Sunset!

From the Unknown God, protect me! From the
Unknown Demon, protect me! From the
Unknown Enemy, protect me! From the
Unknown Sorcery, protect me! From the
Waters of KUTULU, protect me!

From the Wrath of ERESHKIGAL, protect me!
From the Swords of KINGU, protect me!
From the Baneful Look, the Baneful Word, the Baneful Name, the Baneful Number, the Baneful Shape, protect me!
Be watchful, Spirit of the Western Ways, and Remember!

Spirit of the West Gate, Remember!

The Invocation of the Four Gates

MER SIDI!

MER KURRA!
MER URULU!
MER MARTU!
ZI DINGIR ANNA KANPA!
ZI DINGIR KIA KANPA!
UTUK XUL, TA ARDATA!
KUTULU, TA ATTALAKLA!
AZAG-THOTH, TA KALLA!
IA ANU! IA ENLIL! IA NNGI!
ZABAO!

Here follows several particular invocations, for summoning various Powers and Spirits. There may be Words of Necromantic Art, by which it is desirous to speak with the Phantom of someone dead, and perhaps dwelling in ABSU, and thereby a servant of ERESHKIGAL, in which case the Preliminary Invocation that follows is to be used, which is the Invocation used by the Queen of Life, INANNA, at the time of her Descent into that Kingdom of Woe. It is no less then the Opening of the Gate of Ganzir, that leads to the Seven Steps into the frightful Pit. Therefore, do not be alarmed at the sights and sounds that will issue forth from that Opening, for they will be the wails and laments of the Shades that are chained therein, and the shrieking of the Mad God on the Throne of Darkness.

PRELIMINARY INVOCATION OF THE OPERATION OF CALLING OF THE SPIRITS OF THE DEAD WHO DWELL IN CUTHA, OF THE LOST.

BAAD ANGARRU!

NINNGHIZHIDDA!
Thee I invoke, Serpent of the Deep!
Thee I invoke, NINNGHIZHIDDA, Horned Serpent of the Deep!
Thee I invoke, Plumed Serpent of the Deep!
NINNGHIZHIDDA!

Open!
Open the Gate that I may enter!
NINNGHIZHIDDA, Spirit of the Deep, Watcher of the Gate, Remember!
In the Name of our Father, ENKI, before the Flight, Lord and Master of Magicians, Open the Gate that I may enter!

Open, lest I attack the Gate! Open,
lest I break down its bars! Open,
lest I attack the Walls! Open, lest I
leap over It by force!

Open the Gate, lest I cause the Dead to rise and devour the Living!
Open the Gate, lest I give the Dead power over the Living!

Open the Gate, lest I make the Dead to outnumber the Living!
NINNGHIZHIDDA, Spirit of the Deep, Watcher of the Gate, Open!
May the Dead rise and smell the incense!

*And when the Spirit of the on called appears, do not be frightened at his Shape of
condition, but say to him these words*

UUG UDUUG UUGGA GISHTUGBI

*and he will put on a comely appearance, and will answer truthfully all the questions you
shall put to him, which he has writ to answer.*

And it must be remembered that, after the questions have been answered to satisfaction,
the Spirit is to be sent back to whence it came and not detained any longer, and no
attempt must be made to free the Spirit, for that is in violation of the Covenant, and will
bring upon thee and thy generations a most potent curse, wherefore it is unlawful to move
the bones of the Dead or to disinter the bones of the Dead. And the Spirit may be sent
back by means of these words

BARRA UUG UDUUG UUGGA!

*and he will immediately disappear and return to his resting place. If he does not go at
once, simply recite again those words, and he will do so.*

The following is the Great Conjuration of All the Powers, to be used only in extreme
necessity, or to silence a rebellious spirit who plagues thee, or who causeth consternation
about the MANDAL for reasons unknown to thee, perhaps as agent for the Ancient Ones. In
such a case, it is urgent to send back the Spirit before it gains Power by dwelling in the
Upper World, for as long as one of these is present upon the Earth, it gains in strength and
Power until it is almost impossible to control them, as they are unto Gods.

This is the Conjuration, which thou recite forcefully:

THE GREAT CONJURATION OF ALL THE POWERS

SPIRIT OF THE SKY, REMEMBER!

SPIRIT OF THE EARTH, REMEMBER!

Spirits, Lords of the Earth, Remember!

Spirits, Ladies of the Earth, Remember!

Spirits, Lords of the Air Remember!

Spirits, Ladies of the Air, Remember!
Spirits, Lords of the Fire, Remember!
Spirits, Ladies of the Fire, Remember!
Spirits, Lords of the Water, Remember!
Spirits, Ladies of the Water, Remember!
Spirits, Lords of the Stars, Remember!
Spirits, Ladies of the Stars, Remember! Spirits,
Lords of all hostilities, Remember! Spirits, Ladies
of all hostilities, Remember! Spirits, Lords of all
peacefulness, Remember! Spirits, Ladies all
peacefulness, Remember!

Spirits, Lords of the Veil of Shadows, Remember!
Spirits, Ladies of the Veil of Shadows, Remember!
Spirits, Lords of the Light of Life, Remember! Spirits,
Ladies of the Light of Life, Remember! Spirits, Lords of
the Infernal Regions, Remember! Spirits, Ladies of the
Infernal Regions, Remember! Spirits, Lords of the Lords
of MARDUK, Remember! Spirits, Ladies of the Lords of
MARDUK, Remember!
Spirits, Lords of SIN, Who maketh his ship cross the River, Remember!
Spirits, Ladies of SIN, Who maketh his ship cross the skies, Remember!
Spirits, Lords of SHAMMASH, King of the Elder Ones, Remember!

Spirits, Ladies of SHAMMASH GULA, Queen of the Elder Ones, Remember!
Spirits, Lords of TSHKU, Lord of the ANNUNAKI, Remember!
Spirits, Ladies of the Goddess ZIKU, Mother of ENKI, Remember!
Spirits, Lords of NINNASU, Our Father of the Numerous Waters, Remember!
Spirits, Ladies of NINNUAH, Daughter of ENKI, Remember!
Spirits, Lords of NINNGHIZHIDDA, Who upheaves the face of the Earth, Remember!
Spirits, Ladies of NINNISI ANA, Queen of Heaven Remember!
Spirits, Lords and Ladies of the Fire, GIBIL, Ruler Supreme on the Face of the Earth,
Remember!

Spirits of the Seven Doors of the World, Remember!
Spirits of the Seven Locks of the World, Remember! Spirit
KHUSBI KURK, Wife of NAMMTAR, Remember!

Spirit KHITIM KURUKU, Daughter of the Ocean, Remember!

SPIRIT OF THE SKY, REMEMBER!

SPIRIT OF THE EARTH, REMEMBER!

AMANU!

AMANU!
AMANU!

Here endeth the Great Conjuration.

THE CONJURATION OF IA ADU EN I

(A great Mystical Conjuration)

IA IA IA!

ADU EN I BA NINIB
NINIB BA FIRIK
FIRIK BA PIRIK
PIRIK BA AGGA BA ES
AGGA BA ES BA AKKA BAR!
AKKA BAR BA AKKA BA ES
AKKA BA ES BA AKKA BAR
AKKA BAR BA AGGA BA ES
AGGA BA ES BA PIRIK
PIRIK BA FIRIK
FIRIK BE NINIB
NINIB BA ADU EN I
IAIAIAIA!
KUR BUR IA!
EDIN BA EGA
ERIM BA EGURA
E! E! E!
IA IA IA!
EKHI IAK SAKKAK

EKHI AZAG-THOTH
EKHI ASARU
EKHI CUTHALU
IA! IA! IA!

WHAT SPIRITS MAY BE USEFUL

In the Ceremonies of Calling, any type of Spirit may be summoned and detained until It has answered your questions or provided you with whatever you desire. The Spirits of the Dead may be invoked. The Spirits of the Unborn may be invoked. The Spirits of the Seven Spheres may be invoked. The Spirits of the Flame may be invoked. In all, there may be One Thousand-and-One Spirits that are of principal importance, and these you will come to know in the course of your experiments. There are many others, but some have no power, and will only confuse.

The best Spirits to summon in the early Rites are the Fifty Spirits of the Names of Lord MARDUK who give excellent attendance and who are careful Watchers of the Outside. They should not be detained any longer than is necessary, and some are indeed violent

and impatient natures, and their task is to be given in as short a time as possible, and then they are to be released.

After these, the Spirits of the seven Spheres may be invoked to advantage, after the Priest has already trod their Ways after the manner of the Walking. After the Priest has gained Entrance to the gate of NANNA, he may summon the Spirits of that Realm, but not before. These things you will learn in the course of your journey, and it is not necessary to put it all down here, save for a few noble formulae concerning the works of the Sphere of LIBAT, of ISHTAR, the Queen.

These are Works of the gentle passions, which seek to engender affection between man and woman. And they may best be done in a Circle of white, the Priest being properly cleansed and in a clean robe.

Preliminary Purification Invocation

Bright One of the Heavens, wise ISHTAR

Mistress of the Gods, whose "yes" is truly "yes"

Proud One among the Gods, whose command is supreme
Mistress of Heaven and of Earth, who rules in all places
ISHTAR, at your Name all heads are bowed down
I . . . son of . . . have bowed down before you
May my body be purified like lapis lazuli!
May my face be bright like alabaster!
Like shining silver and reddish gold may I not be dull!

To Win the Love of a Woman

(chant the following three times over an apple or a pomegranate; give the fruit to the woman to drink of the juices, and she will surely come to you.)

MUNUS SIGSIGGA AG BARA YE

INNIN AGGISH XASHXUR GISHNU URMA
SHAZIGA BARA YE
ZIGASHUBBA NA AGSISHAMAZIGA
NAMZA YE INNIN DURRE ESH AKKI
UGU AGBA ANDAGUB!

To Recover Potency

(Tie thee knots in a harp string; entwine around both right and left hands, and chant the following incantation seven times, and potency will return.)

LILLIK IM LINU USH KIRI

LISHTAKSSIR ERPETUMMA TIKU LITTUK
NI YISH LIBBI IA LU AMESH ID GINMESH
ISHARI LU SAYAN SAYAMMI YE
LA URRADA ULTU MUXXISHA!

THE CROWN OF ANU OF CALLING

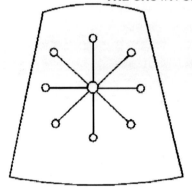

THE FRONTLET OF CALLING

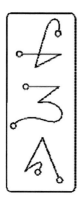

THE COPPER DAGGER OF INANNA OF CALLING

THE SEAL OF THE NORTH GATE

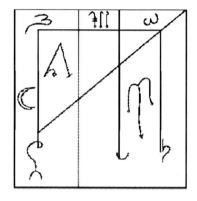

THE SEAL OF THE EAST GATE

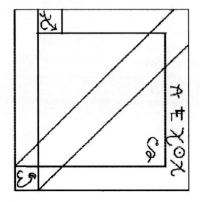

THE SEAL OF THE SOUTH GATE

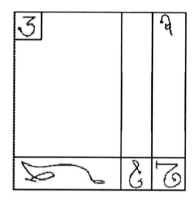

THE SEAL OF THE WEST GATE

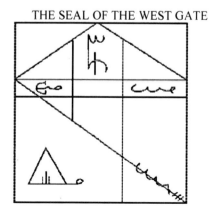

ONE TYPE OF MANDAL OF CALLING

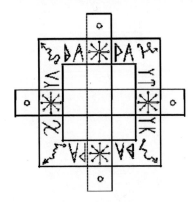

ANOTHER TYPE

Al Azif - The Cipher Manuscript known as
"Necronomicon"

Al Azif *Ye Book of Ye Arab, Abdul Alhazred, 730 at*
Damascus

Of Ye Old Ones and their Spawn

The Old Ones were, the Old Ones are and the Old Ones shall be. From the dark stars They came ere man was born, unseen and loathsome They descended to primal earth.

Beneath the oceans They brooded while ages past, till seas gave up the land, whereupon They swarmed forth in Their multitudes and darkness ruled the Earth.

At the frozen Poles They raised mighty cities, and upon high places the temples of Those whome nature owns not and the Gods have cursed.

And the spawn of the Old Ones covered the Earth, and Their children endureth throughout the ages. Ye shantaks of Leng are the work of Their hands, the Ghasts who dwelleth in Zin's primordial vaults know Them as their Lords. They have fathered the

Na-Hag and the Gaunts that ride the Night; Great Cthulhuis Their brother, the shaggoths Their slaves. The Dholes do homage unto Them in the nighted vale of Pnoth and Gugs sing Their praises beneath the peaks of ancient Throk.

They have walked amidst the stars and They have walked the Earth. The City of Irem in the great desert has known Them; Leng in the Cold Waste has seen Their passing, the timeless citadel upon the cloud-vieled heights of unknown Kadath beareth Their mark.

Wantonly the Old Ones trod the ways of darkness and Their blasphemies were great upon the Earth; all creation bowed beneath Their might and knew Them for Their wickedness.

And the Elder Lords opened Their eyes and beheld the abominations of Those that ravaged the Earth. In Their wrath They set their hand against the Old Ones, staying Them in the midst of Their iniquity and casting Them forth from the Earth to the Void beyond the planes where chaos reigns and form abideth not. And the Elder Lords set Their seal upon the Gateway and the power of the Old Ones prevailest not against its might.

Loathsome Cthulhu rose then from the deeps and raged with exceeding great fury against the Earth Guardians. And They bound his venomous claws with potent spells and sealed him up within the City of R'lyeh wherein beneath the waves he shall sleep death's dream until the end of the Aeon.

Beyond the Gate dwell now the Old Ones; not in the spaces known unto men but in the angles betwixt them. Outside Earth's plane They linger and ever awaite the time of Their return; for the Earth has known Them and shall know Them in time yet to come.

And the Old Ones hold foul and formless Azathoth for Their Master abd Abide with Him in the black cavern at the centre of all infinity, where he gnaws ravenously in ultimate chaos amid the mad beating of hidden drums, the tuneless piping of hideous flutes and the ceaseless bellowing of blind idiot gods that shamble and gesture aimlessly for ever.

The soul of Azathoth dwelleth in Yog-sothoth and He shall beckon unto the Old Ones when the stars mark the time of Their coming; for Yog-sothoth is the Gate through which Those of the Void will re-enter. Yog-sothoth knowest the mazes of of time, for all time is one unto Him. He knowest where the Old Ones came forth in time along long past and where They shall come forth again when the cycle returneth.

After day cometh night; man's day shall pass, and They shall rule where They once ruled. As foulness you shall know them and Their accursedness shall stain the Earth.

Of Ye Times and Ye Seasons to be Observed

Whenever thou would'st call forth Those from Outside, thou must mark well the seasons and times in which the spheres do intersect and the influences flow from the Void

Thou must observe the cycle of the Moon, the movements of the planets, the Sun's course

through the Zodiac and the rising of the constellations.

Ye Ultimate Rites shall be performed only in the seasons proper to them, these be: at Candlemas (on the second day of the second month), at Beltane (on the Eve of May), at Lammas (on the first day of the eighth month), at Roodmas (on the fourteenth day of the ninth month), and at Hallowmas (on November Eve).

Call out to dread Azathoth when the Sun is in the sign of the Ram, the Lion, or the Archer; the Moon decreasing and Mars and Saturn conjoin.

Mighty Yog-sothoth shall rise to ye incantations when Sol has entered the fiery house of Leo and the hour of Lammas be upon ye.

Evoke ye terrible Hastur on Candlemas Night, when Sol is in Aquarius and Mercury in trine.

Supplicate Great Cthulhu only at Hallowmas Eve when the Sun abides within the House of the Scorpion and Orion riseth. When All Hallows falls within the cycle of the new Moon the power shall be the strongest.

Conjure Shub-Niggurath when the Beltane fires glow upon the hills and the Sun is in the Second House, repeating the Rites of Roodmas when ye Black One appeareth.

To Raise up Ye Stones

To form ye Gate through which They from ye Outer Void might manifest thou must set up ye stones in ye elevenfold configuration.

First thou shalt raise up ye four cardinal stones and these shall mark ye direction of ye four winds as they howleth through their seasons.

To ye North set ye the stone of Great Coldness that shall form ye Gate of ye winter-wind engraving thereupon the sigil of the Earth-Bull thus:{Taurus sigil}

In ye South (at a space of five paces from ye stone of ye North), thou shalt raise a stone of fierce-heat, through which ye summer winds bloweth and make upon ye stone ye mark of ye Lion-serpent thus:{Leo Sigil}

Ye stone of whirling-air shall be set in ye East where ye first equinox riseth and shall be graven with ye sign of he that beareth ye waters, thus:{Aquarius Sigil}

Ye Gate of Rushing Torrents thou cause to beat the west most inner point (at a space of five paces from ye stone of ye East) where ye sun dieth in ye evening and ye cycle of night returns. Blazon ye stone with ye character of ye Scorpion whose tail reacheth unto the stars:{Scorpio Sigil}

Set thou the seven stones of Those that wander ye heavens, without ye inner four and

through their diverse influences shall ye focus of power be established.

In ye North beyond the stone of Great Coldness set ye first ye stone of Saturn at a space of three paces. This being done proceed thou widdershins placing at like distances apart ye stones of Jupiter, Mercury, Mars, Venus, Sul and Luna marking each with their rightful sign.

At ye center of the so completed configuration set ye the Alter of ye Great Old Ones and seal it with ye symbol of Yog-Sothoth and ye mighty Names of Azathoth, Cthulhu, Hastur, Shub-Niggurath and Nyarlathotep.

And ye stones shall be ye Gates through which thou shalt call Them forth from Outside man's time and space.

Entreat ye of ye stones by night and when the Moon decreasetth in her light, turning thy face to ye direction of Their coming, speaking ye words and making ye gestures that bringeth forth ye Old Ones and causeth Them to walk once more ye Earth.

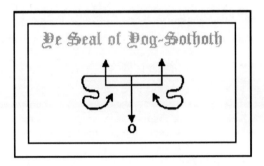

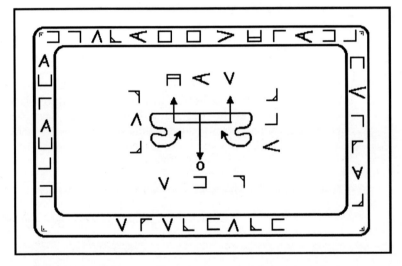

Of Diverse Signs

These most potent signs shall be so formed with thy left hand when thou employeth them in ye Rites

Ye first sign is that of Voor and in nature it be ye true symbol of ye Old Ones. Make ye thus whenever thou wouldst supplicate Those that ever waite beyond the Threshold.

Ye second sign is that of Kish and it breaketh down all barriers and openeth ye portals of ye Ultimate Planes.

In ye third place goeth ye Great Sign of Koth which sealeth ye Gates and guardeth ye pathways.

Ye Signs of Power

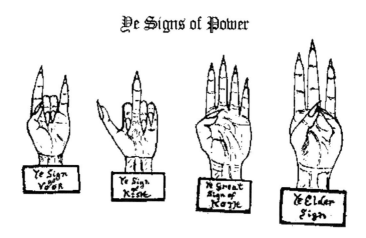

Ye forth sign is that of ye Elder Gods. It protecteth those who would evoke ye powers by night, and banish ye forces of menace and antagonism.

(Nota: Ye Elder Sign hath yet another form and when so enscribed upon ye grey stone of Mnar it serveth to hold back ye power of Ye Great Old Ones for all time.)

Ye Elder Sign

Ye Sign of Koth , engraved

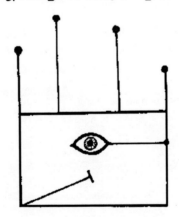

To Compound Ye Incense of Zkauba

In the day and hour of Mercury with the Moon in her increase, thou shalt
take equal parts of Myrrh, Civet, Storax, Wormwood, Assafoetida,
Galbanum and Musk, mix well together and reduce all to the finest powder.

Place the so assembled elements in a vessel of green glass and seal with a brazen stopper afore inscribed with the characters of Mars and Saturn.

Elevate the vessel to the Four Winds and cry aloud the supreme words of

power thus: To the North: *ZIJMUORSOBET, NOIJM, ZAVAXO!*

To the East: *QUEHAIJ, ABAWO, NOQUETONAIJI!*

To the South: *OASAIJ, WURAM, THEFOTOSON!*

To the West: *ZIJORONAIFWETHO, MUGELTHOR, MUGELTHOR-YZXE!*

Cover the vessel with a cloth of black velvet and set aside.

For each of seven nights thou shalt bathe the vessel in Moonlight for the space of one hour - keeping it concealed beneath the cloth from cock-crow till sunset.

All this being accomplished the incense shall be ready for use and possessed of such vertue that he that useth it with knowledge shall have power to call forth and command the Infernal Legions.

Nota: When employed in ye Ultimate Rites the incense may be rendered more efficacious by the addition of one part powdered mummy-Egypticus.

Employ the perfume of Zkauba in all ceremonies of ye ancient Lore casting ye essences upon live coals of Yew or Oak. And when ye spirits drawn near, the vaporous smoke shall enchant and fascinate them, binding their powers to thy will.

{Editor's Note: In the published edition a series of planetary glyphs and sigils are shown in reference to the above formula. These have been omitted as they are not illustrated in the original manuscript but were provided from other unrelated texts by the publishers.}

To Make Ye Powder of Ibn Ghazi

THE MYSTIC POWDER OF MATERIALIZATION:

Take ye dust of ye tomb - wherein ye body has lain for two hundred years or more past -, three parts. Take of powdered Amaranth, two parts; of ground Ivy leaf, one part, and of fine salt, one part.

Compound all together in an open mortar in the day and hour of Saturn.

Make over the thus assembled ingredients the Voorish sign, and then seal up the powder within a leaden casket whereupon is graven the sigil of Koth.

YE USING OF YE POWDER:

Whenever thou wisheth to observe the airial manifestations of the spirits blow a pinch of ye powder in the irection of their coming, either from the palm of thy hand or the blade of the Magic Bolyne.

Mark ye well that ye maketh ye Elder Sign at their appearence, lest the tendrils of darkness enter thy soul.

Ye Unction of Khephnes Ye Egyptian

Whosoever anointeth his head with the ointment of Khephnes shall in sleep be grabted true visions of time yet to come

When ye Moon increaseth in her light place in an earthen crucible a goodly quantity of oil of ye Lotus, sprinkle with one once powdered mandragora and stir well with ye forked twig of ye wild thorn bush. Having so done utter ye incantation of Yebsu (taken fron diverse lines in ye papyrus) thus:

I am the Lord of

Spirits,

Oridimbai,

Sonadir,

Episghes,

I am Ubaste, Ptho born of Binui

Sphe, Phas; In the name of

Auebothiabathabaithobeuee Give

power to my spell O Nasira

Oapkis Shfe,

Give power Chons-in-Thebes-Nefer-

hotep, Ophois, Give power! O

Bakaxikhekh!

Add to ye potion pinch of red earth, nine drops natron, for drops balsam of Olibanum and one drop blood (from thy right hand). Combine the whole with a like measure of fat of the gosling and place ye vessel upon ye fire. When all is rendered well and ye dark vapours begin to rise, make ye the Elder Sign and remove from ye flames.

When the unguent has cooled place it within an urn of ye finest alabaster, which thou shalt keep in some secret place (known only to thyself) until thou shalt have need of it.

To Fashion the Scimitar of Barzai

In the day and hour of Mars and when the Moon increaseth, make thou the scimitar of bronze with a hilt of fine ebony.

Upon one side of the the blade thou shalt enscribe these characters:

{Editor's Note: These graphics are not shown in the

Manuscript} And upon the other side these:

{Editor's Note: These graphics are not shown in the Manuscript}

On the day and hour of Saturn the moon decreasing, light thou a fire of
Laurel and yew boughs and offering the blade to the flames pronounce the
five-fold conjuration thus:

HCORIAXOJU, ZODCARNE

SI powerfully call upon ye and stir ye up O ye mighty

spirits that dwelleth in the Great Abyss.

In the dread and potent name of AZATHOTH come ye forth and give power
unto this blade fashioned in accordance to ancient Lore.

*By **XENTHON O-ROHMATR U** I command you **O AZIABELI S** by*
***YSEHYROROSET H** I call the O **ANTIQUELI S** and in the Vast and*
*Terrible Name of **DAMAMIAC H**that Crom-yha uttered and the mountains*
*shook I mightily compel ye forth O **BARBUELI S**, attend me! aid me! give*
power unto my spell that this weapon that bearest the runes of fire recieveth
such vertue that it shall strike fear into the hearts of all spirits that would
disobey my commands, and that it shall assist me to form all manner of
Circles, figures and mystic sigils necessary in the operations of Magickal Art.

*In the Name of Great and Mighty **YO G-SOTHOTH**and in the invincible sign*
of Voor

(Give Sign)

Give Power Give Power Give Power

When the flames turn blue it shall be a sure sign that the spirits obey your
demands whereupon thou shalt quench the blade in an afore prepared
mixture of brine and cock- gall.

Burn the incense of Zkauba as an offering to the spirits thou hast called forth, then dismiss them to their abodes with these words:

*In the Names of **AZATHOTH**and **YO G-SOTHOTH** Their servant **NYARLATHOTEP** and by the power of this sign* (make ye the Elder Sign), *I discharge thee; go forth from this place in peace and return ye not until I calleth thee.* (Seal ye portals with the sign of Koth).

Wrap the scimitar in a cloth of black silk and setit aside until thou wouldst make use of it; but mark ye well that no other shall lay his hand upon the scimitar lest its vertue be forever lost.

{Editor's Note: The following graphic alphabet is deciphered from the manuscript, according to the publishers, by use of a "Magic Square Cipher" inherent in the   manuscript itself and is therefor included in this etext version.}

Ye Alphabet of NugSoth

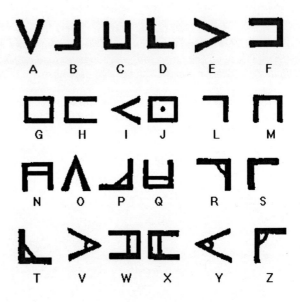

(Note: In ye writing of ye mystic runes of Nug-Soth ye latin C serveth for ye K.)

Ye characters of Nug hold ye key to ye planes, employ ye them in ye talismanic art and in all ye sacred inscriptions

Ye Voice of Hastur

Hear ye the Voice of dread Hastur, hear the mournful sigh of the vortex, the mad rushing of the Ultimate Wind that Swirls darkly amongst the silent stars.

Hear ye Him that howls serpent-fanged amid the bowels of nether earth; He whose ceaseless roaring ever fills the timeless skies of hidden Leng.

His might teareth the forest and crusheth the city, but none shall know the hand that smiteth and the soul that destroys, for faceless and foul walketh the Accursed One, His form to men unknown.

Hear then His Voice in the dark hours, answer His call with thine own; bow ye and pray at His passing, but speak not His name aloud.

Concerning Nyarlathotep

I hear the Crawling Chaos that calls beyond the stars

And They created Nyarlathotep for Their messenger, and They clothed Him with Chaos that His form might be ever hidden amidst the stars.

Who shall know the mystery of Nyarlathotep? for He is the mask and will of Those that were when time was not. He is the priest of the Ether, the Dweller in Air and hath many faces that none shall recall.

The waves freeze before Him; Gods dread His call. In men's dreams He whispers, yet who knoweth His form?

Of Leng in Ye Cold Waste

Who seeketh Northwards beyond the twilight land of Inquanok shall find amidst the frozen waste the dark and mighty plateau of thrice-forbidden Leng.

Know ye time-shunned Leng by the ever-burning evil-fires and ye foul screeching of the scaly Shantak birds which ride the upper air; by the howling of ye Na-hag who brood in nighted caverns and haunt men's dreams with strange madness, and by the grey stone temple beneath the Night Gaunts lair, wherein is he who wears the Yellow Mask and dwelleth all alone.

But beware O Man, beware, of Those who tread in Darkness the ramparts of Kadath, for he that beholds Their mitred-heads shall know the claws of doom.

Of Kadath Ye Unknown

What man knoweth Kadath? For who
shall know of that which ever abides in
strange-time, twix yesterday, today and
the morrow.

Unknown amidst ye Cold Waste lieth the mountain of Kadath where upon the hidden summit an Onyx Castle stands. dark clouds shroud the mighty peak that gleams 'neath ancient stars where silent brood the titan towers and rear forbidden walls.

Curse-runes guard the nighted gate carved by forgotten hands, and woe to he that dare pass within those dreadful doors.

Earth's Gods revel where Others once walked in mystic timeless halls, which some have glimpst in sleeps dim vault through strange and sightless eyes.

To Call Forth YogSothoth

For Yog-Sothoth is

the Gate. He

knoweth where the

Old Ones

came forth in times

past and where They

came forth again when

the cycle
returneth

When thou would call forth Yog-Sothoth thou must waite until the Sun is in the Fifth House with Saturn in trine. Then enter within the stones and draw about thee the Circle of evocation tracing the figurines with the mystic scimitar of Barzai.

Circumambulate thrice widdershins and turning thy face to the South intone the conjuration that openeth the Gate:

Ye
Conjuration

O Thou that dwelleth in the darkness of the Outer Void, come forth unto the Earth once more I entreat thee.

O Thou who abideth beyond the Spheres of Time, hear my

supplication. (Make the sign of Caput Draconis)

O Thou who art the Gate and the Way come forth come forth Thy servant

calleth Thee. (Make the Sign of Kish)

BENATIR! CARARKAU! DEDOS! YOG-SOTHOTH! come forth! come forth! I speak the words, I Break Thy bonds, the seal is cast aside, pass through the Gate and enter the World I maketh Thy mighty Sign!

(Make the Sign of the Voor)

Trace the pentagram of Fire and say the incantation that causeth the Great One to manifest before the Gate:

Ye Incantation

Zyweso, wecato, keoso, Xuneve -rurom Xeverator. Menhatoy, Zywethorosto zuy, Zururogos Yog-Sothoth! Orary Ysgewot, homor athanatos nywe zumquros, Ysechyroroseth Xoneozebethoos Azathoth! Xono, Zuwezet, Quyhet kesos ysgeboth Nyarlathotep!; zuy rumoy quano duzy Xeuerator, YSHETO, THYYM, quaowe xeuerator phoe nagoo, Hastur! Hagathowos yachyros Gaba Sub-Niggurath! meweth, xosoy Vzewoth!

(Make the sign of Cauda Draconis)

TALUBSI! ADULA! ULU! BAACHUR!

Come forth Yog-Sothoth! come forth!

* * *

And then he will come unto thee and bring His Globes and He will give true answer to all you desire to know. And He shall reveal unto you the secret of His seal by which you may gain favour in the sight of the Old Ones when They once more walk the Earth.

* * *

And when His hour be past the curse of the Elder Lords shall be upon Him and draw Him forth beyond the Gate where He shall abide until He be summoned.

Ye Circle of Evocation

North

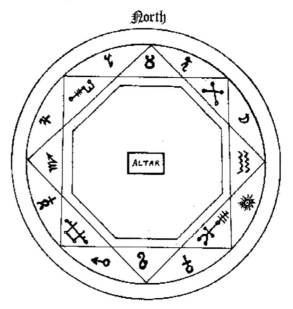

{Editor's Note: Included on this page are a number of sigils and a magic circle. These

illustrations are not in the Manuscript but were referenced from other texts, including, but not limited to; Key of Solomon (see Additional Ms. 36,674, British Museum Library)   and Three Books of Occult Philosophy- Cornelius Agrippa. They are therefor not included in this version.}

To Conjure
of Ye Globes

Know ye that the Globes of Yog-Sothoth be thirteen in number, and they be the powers of the Parasite-hoard which are His servitors and doeth His bidding in ye world.

Call them forth whenever thou shall have need of anything and they shall grant their powers unto ye when ye shall call them with the incantations and make their sign.

His Globes have diverse names and appeareth in many forms.

The first is GOMORY, who appeareth like a camel with a crown of gold upon his head. He commandeth twenty-six legions of infernal spirits and giveth the knowledge of all magical jewels and talismans.

The second splrit is ZAGAN, who appeareth like a great bull, or a King terrible in aspect. Thirty-three legions bow before him and he teacheth the mysteries of the sea.

The Third is called SYTRY, who taketh the form of a great Prince. He hath sixty legions and telleth the secrets of time yet to come.

ELIGOR is the fourth spirit; he appeareth like a red man with a crown of iron upon his head. He commandeth likewise sixty legions and giveth the knowledge of victory in war, and telleth of strife to come.

The fifth spirit is called DURSON and hath with him twenty-two familiar demons and appeareth like a raven. He can reveal all occult secrets and tell of past times.

The sixth is VUAL his form is of a dark cloud and he teacheth all manner of ancient tongues.

The seventh is SCOR, who appeareth like a white snake, he bringeth money at your command.

ALGOR is the eighth spirit, he appeareth in the likeness of a fly. He can tell of all secret things and granteth the favours of great Princes and Kings.

The ninth is SEFON. He appeareth like a man with a green face and hath the power to show where treasure is hidden.

Tenth is PARTAS, He hath the form of a great vulture, and can tell ye the vertues of herbs, stones, make ye invisible and restore sight which is lost.

The eleventh spirit is GAMOR, and when he appeareth like a man can marvellously enform ye of how to win favours of great persons and can drive away any spirit that

guardeth over treasure.

Twelfth is UMBRA, He appeareth like a giant; he can convey money from place to place if thou bid him and bestow the love of any woman that thou desirest.

The thirteenth spirit is ANABOTH who taketh the form of a yellow toad. He hath the power to make thee marvellous cunning in nigromancy, he can drive away any devil that would hinder ye and tell of strange and hidden things.

* * *

When thou wouldst call up ye Globes thou must first make upon the earth this sign:

Make the Sign of Voor

And evoke
of them
thus:

EZPHARES, OLYARAM, IRIN -ESYTION, ERYONA, OREA, ORASYM, MOZIM!

By these words and in the name of YOG-SOTHOTH who is thy master, I do most powerfully summon and call ye up O .... N .... That thou mayest aid me in my hour of need.

Come forth I command ye by the

sign of Power! (Make the sign of

Voor)

* * *

And then the spirit shall appear unto thee and grant thy requests.

But if he remaineth invisible to thine eye, blow the dust of Ibn Ghazi and he will immediately take his proper form.

When thou wouldst banish what ye have called up eraze thou their sign with the scimitar of Barzai and utter the words:

CALDULECH ! DALMALEY ! CADAT !

(and seal with the sign of Koth).

Nota: If on their appearance the spirits obstinately refuse to speak cleave the air thrice

with the scimitar and say: ADRICANOROM DUMASO! And their tongue shall be loosened and they will be compelled to give true answer.

Ye Adjuration of
Great Cthulhu

Ph'nglui mglw'nafh Cthulhu R'lyeh Wgah'nagl fhtan.

A supplication to great Cthulhu for those who would have power over his minions.

In the day and hour of the moon with sun in scorpio prepare thou a waxen tablet and enscribe thereon the seals of Cthulhu and Dagon; suffumigate with the incense of Zkauba and set aside.

On Hallowmas eve thou must travel to some lonely place where high ground overlooks the ocean. Take up the tablet in thy right hand and make of the sign of Kish with thy left. Recite the incantation thrice and when the final word of the third utterance dieth in the air cast thou the tablet into the waves saying:

'In His House at R'lyeh Dead Cthulhu waits dreaming, yet He shall rise and His kingdom shall cover the Earth.'

And He shall come unto you in sleep and show His sign with which ye shall
unlock the   secrets of the deep.

Ye Incantation

O Thou that lieth dead but ever
dreameth, Hear, Thy servant
calleth Thee .

Hear me O
mighty Cthulhu !
' Hear me Lord
of Dreams !

In Thy tower at R'lyeh They have
sealed ye , but Dagon shall break
Thy accursed bonds , and Thy
Kingdom shall rise once more .
The Deep Ones knoweth Thy
secret Name , The Hydra
knoweth Thy lair ;
Give forth Thy sign that I
may kno w Thy will upon
the Earth .
When death dies, Thy time
shall be , and Thou shalt
sleep no more ;
Grant me the power to still
the waves , that I may
hear Thy Call .

(At ye third repeating of ye incantation cast forth the Tablet into ye waves
saying):

In His House at R'lyeh Dead Cthulhu waits dreaming, yet He shall rise and
His kingdom shall cover the Earth.

Ye Tablet of R'lyeh

To Summon Shub-Niggurath Ye Black

Where the stones have been set up thou shalt call out to Shub- Niggurath, and unto he that knoweth the signs and uttereth the words all earthly pleasures shall be granted.

* * *

When the sun entereth the Sign of the Ram and the time of night is upon ye turn thy face to the North wind and read the verse aloud:

> *Iah ! SHUB-*
> *NIGGURATH !*
> *Great Black Goat of*
> *the.Woods , I Call*
> *Thee forth !*
> *(Kneel)*

Answer the cry of thy
servan t who knoweth
the words of power !
(make the Voorish sign
)
Rise up I say from thy
slumber s and come forth
with a thousand more !
(make the sign of Kish
)
I make the signs, I speak
the word s that openeth
the door !
Come forth I say, I
turn the Key , Now !
walk the Earth once
more !

Cast the perfumes upon the coals, trace the sigil of Blaesu and pronounce the words of power:

Make the Sign of Koth

ZARIATNATMIX, JANNA,

ETITNAMUS, HAYRAS,

FABELLERON, FUBENTRONTY,

BRAZO, TABRASOL, NISA,

VARF-SHUB-NIGGURATH ! GABOTS MEMBROT !

And then the Black one shall come forth unto thee and the thousand Horned Ones who howl shall rise up from the Earth. And thou shalt hold before them the talisman of Yhe upon which they shall bow to thy power and answer thy demands.

When thou would banish those that you have called forth intone the words:

IMAS, WEGHAYMNKO, QUAHERS, XEWEFARAM

Which closeth the Gate, and seal with the
sign of Koth.

Ye Formula of Dho-Hna

Whosoever performeth this Rite with true understanding shall pass beyond
ye Gates of Creation and enter ye Ultimate Abyss wherein dwelleth ye
vapourous Lord S'ngac who eternally pondereth ye Mystery of Chaos.

Trace ye Angle-Web with ye Scimitar of Barzai and offer the mystic
suffumigations with

the incense of Zkauba.

Enter ye Web by the Gate of the North and reciting the incantation of Na
(thus): ZAZAS, NASATANADA, ZAZAS ZAZAS, proceed to ye South-
most Pinnacle by the Path of Alpha whereupon make ye, ye Sign of Kish,
pronouncing the triple-Word of power thrice, (thus so): OHODOS-SCIES-

ZAMONI! proceed thence to ye Angle of the North- East chanting the third verse of ye Fifth Psalm of Nyarla- thotep seglecting not to make the quintuple genuflection on passing through ye curve locus-(thus):

The All-One dwelleth in Darkness, At the centre of All dwelleth He that is the Darkness; And tfiat Darkness shall be eternal when all shall bow before the Onyx Throne.

Pause at the Third Angle and make ye once more the Sign of Kish speaking the words that clear the portal and stay the course of time: ABYssus-D|AcoNrsus, ZEXOWE- AZATHOTH!) NRRGO, IAA! NYAR-LATHOTEP!

Follow the Third Path to the Pinnacle of the West and there perform the obeisances in silence (bow low thrice and give the gesture of Voor). Turn and tread the Path of Transfiguration leading to ye Ultimate Angle. Open up the Abyss Gate by the ninefold affirmation (thus): ZENOXESE, PIOTH, OXAS ZAEGOS, MAVOC NIGORSUS, BAYAR! HEECHO! YOG-SOTHOTH! YOG-SOTHOTH! YOG-SOTHOTH!

Ye Sigil of Transformation

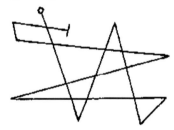

Make ye the Sigil of Transformation and step thou forth into ye Gulf.

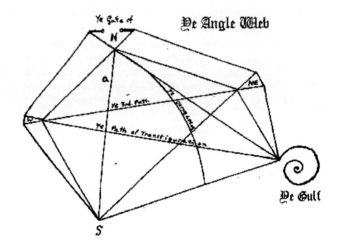

Ye Gate of   Ye Angle Web

N

a

NE

Ye 3rd Path

Ye Path of Transfiguration

W

Ye Gulf

S

THE R'LYEH TEXT

Hidden Leaves From The Necronomicon

Their Hidden Place

I have seen much unmeant for mortal eyes in my wanderings beneath that dark and forgotten city. It is not the splendours of Irem that haunt my dreams with this madness, but another place, a place shrouded in utter silence; long unknown to man and shunned even by ghoul and nightgaunt. A stillness likened to millions of vanished years pressed with great heaviness upon my soul as I trod those labyrinths in terror, ever fearing that my footfalls might awaken the dread architects of this nameless region where the hand of time is bound and the wind does not whisper   .

Great was my fear of this place, but greater was the strange slee

-like fascination that gripped my

mind and guided my feet ever downwards through realms unknown. My lamp cast it's radiance upon basalt walls, revealing mighty pillars hewn surely by no human hand, where curiously stained obelisks engraved with frightful images and cryptic characters reared above me into the darkness. A passage sloped before me, I descended. For what seemed to be an eternity I descended rapt in contemplation of the grim icons that stretched endlessly on either hand, depicting the strange deeds of Those Great Ones born not of mortal womb. They had dwelt here and passed on, yet the walls of the edifice bore Their mark: vast likenesses of those terrible beings of yore carved beneath a firmament of unguessed asterisms.

Endlessly the way led downwards, ever downwards. The passage of time had fled from my mind, Hypnos and eternity held my soul .

How long, how far had I journeyed? I knew not. Then like one awaking from the dreams of Narcaeus my eyes beheld a door which barred my path. Their Sign was upon it, The Sign which I have seen within the tom bcaverns of Leng, amidst the pillars of Irem , and borne before the idols of cryptic Isnavor. I trembled as I beheld the dark inscriptions which covered the jaded stone writhe like a thousand hideous serpents, sometimes their reptilian forms darting toward each other as if in conflict, sometimes joining to form creatures of nauseous bulk once more to divide into a twisting host of black serpentine characters .

Before my eyes the door was rolled up as if it were a scroll and I gazed upon the void beyond, where amongst strange stars great darkling forms moved. Like the moaning of a great wind terrible voices

assailed my ears with a cry of a thousand souls in torment. The forbidden names of Yog-Sothoth

Cthulhu, Nyarlathhotep and a hundred more seared my brain like venomous vitriol. Their minds entered my being and I learned of blasphemous things undreamt by mortal man and of a realm beyond our time and creation where the blind demon sultan Azathoth dwells within the pit of Chaos throughout the countless aeons of infinity   .

Then with thunderous roar the stars whirled before me in a great coiling vortex and I was drawn into that nameless abyss like a leaf before the tempest . My screams of terror yielded to merciful oblivion and darkness engulfed me .

I awoke amidst the silent sands of the red desert to behold the great orb of the sun proclaiming the dawn. I arose, and turning to the North set my feet towards

Damascus where I, Their scribe, must write my book. For beyond the Pillars of
Hercules, dreaming crystals call   .

Of He Who Sleeps

Know ye that He has slept death's dream for ages unnumbered; He who has
slumbered long before the birth of Man; He who is dead yet waits dreaming:
SHALL RISE, and His time draws near. The worm shall not corrupt the corrupted;
time is naught to His continuation; the aeons shall not lay waste that which is not
o €arth's flesh .

In R'Lyeh He dwells, bound in timeless sleep by Those who would hold back the
darkness of Outer Hells and stem the fate of Man. Yet the darkness shall prevail,
the destiny of Man is sealed and graven .

The stars shall mark the time of His coming, and when the spheres intersect: HE
SHALL RISE. Great Cthulhu shall return, and armed with vengeful talons He
shall smite the Elder Lords and rend the soul of Man. The earth shall know the
night without cease   .

His minions dwell amongst you, Beware O Man, they come in servile stealth;
like thieves in the night. They heed not Man and his frail gods, blind in the
will of their master   .

*Great Cthulhu sleeps in His house and shapes the dream of what shall me, dead
Cthulhu waits dreaming.*

My brother Ibn Ghazi saw with the lidless eyes the end of Man's time, yet Their curse
denied him the revelation. Ever condemned he suffers the endless torments of the
Vaults of Zin. His mouth is sealed

up, his tongue severe & nought shall he speak or bewail his torture Shoggoth until the
Great Old Ones fall   .

- he is headless, the slave of the

Yog-Sothoth knoweth the Gate through which the Old Ones shall return. When the
stars have faded and the moon shines no more, when only dark suns rise and set:
Great Cthulhu shall awaken and call from the deep with the voice of a thousand
thunders, and the Gate shall be cast open: THEY SHALL RETURN .

Lament thy fate O Man, for the earth shall be void and cast for eternity into the abyss of perdition

. IN HIS TOMB AT R'LYEH GREAT CTHULHU DREAMS .

The Seal They have set against Him shall not prevail forever. The folly of mankind shall shatter the Seal: HE SHALL RISE .

Man in his unseeing ignorance shall assault the skein which binds his immortality (and know not who guides his hand); he shall rupture the air and oceans with fire, and cover the firmament with the venomous shroud of ancient Cthulhu's shadow .

I, Alhazred, have heard His cry, my eyes have beheld the forbidden Signs, I fear the voice of the night win d- I fear for man .

Ph'hglui mglw'nafh Cthulhu R'lyeh Wgah'nagl fhta   n

The Nurturing Of The Cadaver

What hand harvests the soul at death?

What dwells within the tomb after the spirit has

departed? What locks the Gate beneath the

serpent's eye?

STANZA 1.

He who would possess the hidden power must pay homage to Those of the Void and provide the sustenance of Their being. In ages past They created bodies of flesh and walked the earth and bred diverse life-forms for Their nourishment: creatures of Their design, (some yet continue upon earth) shaped and coloured to serve Their needs
.

In the Void They dwell without form; Their mantle of flesh long destroyed, yet Their desire for the essence of matter remains and long unremembered lusts burn with ravenous ferocity

When life has fled the corpus the fly of Yoth must be encapsulated thus; Make the incision with the Scimitar of Barzai and over the head of the cadaver pronounce the

Incantation

:

ZECK A-REBUS PRATCHI, RO'KA   S

WELBREBOSDOS SATIGOC INRUT,

YOTH IMBRUT, ZECK AREBUS

YOTH! RO'KAS YOTH !

Make the Voorish Sign and burn the Incense of ZKAUBA   .

Take up a brand of fire and facing to the West pronounce the words: BELUM OSAS GRIMSAL,

BOGAD RITZAS, PEGVIER, LAZOZ IMBRUT, ZECK

-REBUS, YOTH !

Strike the brazen gong and as the sound dies from your ears the insect will attend you and enter the wound. The fly will dwell therein for one hundred and ninety days and from its decay shall rise the nine worms of ISCUXCAR which shall gnaw as instructed until naught remains but the essence

If the N a-hags come forth banish them with the Elder Sign (which they fear greatly) and bar their return with the Amulet Of Iron   .

Thus prepared, the essence may be offered to Those beyond for Their appeasement whenever you shall Open the Gate as before taught. (Make the triple genuflection and Seal with the Sigil of Koth at Their coming) .

The glittering Powder of Desiccation may be formulated from the remains if pulverised in the day and hour of Saturn and combined with the ochre of the earth, salt and sulphur   .

Mummia can be produced by sprinkling the powder upon any corporeal being   .

The Vessel Of Balon

Fashion a vessel in the form of a brazen head. Upon the brow engrave the sigil   :

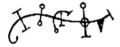

beneath the right eye :

beneath the left eye :

beneath the mouth .

(to the right) and

(to the left) .

Set the vessel upon a stone engraved with the emblems of great Balon. Last, let the eyes of his vessel
be set with obsidian. Seal within the cranium a quantity of the Powder of Ibn Garzi, the metals of the ancient planets and the essence of life .

When the moon is old take the vessel veiled in black to some high place where no man is abroad and turn the countenance to the North. Unveil the head and burn the incense of Zakubar before it. Then you shall call forth five servitors of Balon in His name

:

VEDAL, NOCUSA, IBROS, DENAK, ENPROS I call you forth in the name of your Master: Great BALON! Behold your Signs and look upon this image with favour for this vessel awaits you in silence. I evoke you in these words: KADESES YOLMO REEGUS EMIG ORRESSUS DIZZAG, ORRESSUS, ORRESSUS DIZZAG, and by

the power of His emblems that I have set before you. I bid you enter this vessel
and feast upon the essences you so desire .

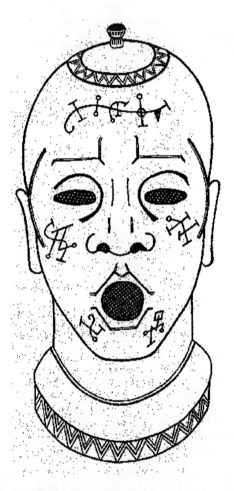

The spirits shall appear as a red vapour before the image, and the essences within the
cranium shall beckon their lust, and they shall enter through the mouth of the vessel.
When they are within make
the sign of KOTH and seal up the mouth with red clay (which you have before prepared)
saying

VOLEC DEMAS, ORIS, through this earth you shall not pass. The words have been spoken, the Sign has been given, for as long as I so will it you shall dwell within this vessel I have fashioned with my Art and thou shall give true answers to my demands when I shall have need of you; for Balon your Master has cast you forth from the hosts that serve Him to be obedient to my will in return for my worship and due sacrifice

Veil the image with black cloth .

When thou wish to know of anything which is hidden from you in the world of man or realm of elemental spiri t- Unveil the head, turn the face to the North, ask what you desire to know and address the image in these words :

"I have fashioned you

with my Art, I have

given you life ,

Now answer in truth. "

(Make the Voorish Sign and burn incense)   .

The Seals of the Vessel must never be broken for the Spirits will seek to destroy you upon their release .

To Fashion The Ring Of Hypnos

The realm of sleep touches earth's world in many places, but it is beyond the mighty Towers of the West that the dreams of man mingle with the threads of eternity. Only there where thought has form and purple Hypnos rules can a waking man tread the Valley of the Land of Sleep and behold the Web of Minds therein .

To enter the dreams of another you must know the Names and Sigils of the four Guardians of this realm and possess the Ring of Passage   .

The four Guardian Spirits of the Western Portal (through which you must pass) each have names of five letters and diverse characters in which the secrets of their power are locked, thus

:

NEMUS:

DACOS:

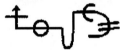

CABID:

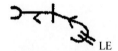

LE

EBO:

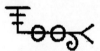

Fashion a ring from virgin silver in the day and hour of Jupiter and engrave upon it these characters

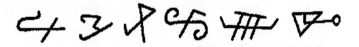

In the day and hour of Mercury furnish the ring with a bezel of bronze bearing this character

:

For one cycle of the Moon expose the Ring to the elements in which time the silver will blacken and the bronze turn green .

In the dark of the Moon write the Names and Sigils of the four Guardians upon the parchment and
suffumigate with storax while calling upon the said Guardians in

these words -: Nemus, Dacos, Cabid, Leebo !

I call you forth by your ancient name   s

Attend me in my work and behold these

your symbols! YAILISBO IBUZOD !

Place the Ring upon the parchment and recite the Incantation in a low voice   :

YOBUS RESUSYARTA NEBEE, RISSANUS NEBEE ZHIYA, VEN
REBUSERIC NI ARDAS ARBAOS VANZEE GEREL ZIMPHANSE
NI NEBEE AWENHATOACORO, VEHATH, HAGATHORWOS.

Sprinkle the ring twice with the juice of juniper mixed with the oil of civet and perfume
with the Incense of Zkauba, saying :

Nemus, Dacos,

Cabid, Leeb o I

bind you in

these words :

ADULAL! ABUIAL! LEBUSHI !

Let me pass before

unhindered Through the

realms of your Kingdom

And let not sleep dim

my eyes .

(Make the Sign of Kish)

Place the Ring and parchment within a leaden casket and set it aside for the space of
seven days

When you have need to enter the drea

-mind of another, in the hours of night place the Ring upon

the second finger of your left hand, turn West and pressing the bezel to your forehead
pronounce the four Names upon the parchment and you shall pass in a moment between
the Towers of the West and enter the realm of sleep. Speak the name of the dreamer and
your minds shall become as one until Morpheus lifts his spell .

The secrets and desires of any an or woman shall be revealed to you through the images
of their dreams. Yet, only those who sleep the hours of the night shall be subject to the
power of the Ring,

for the radiance of the sun utterly destroys it's virtue, and the Key shall be los

- The Spirits are not

answerable to a second calling .

The Amulet Of Nodens

The amulet of Lord Nodens is a Shield of Protection against the fiends that walk
the night; the demonic adversaries that assail Mankind. Whoever shall bear this
Symbol upon his breast shall turn back the legions of darkness until the despoilers
of earth return   .

When the Moon is in her increase and Orion ascends in the East: Take a plate of
purest silver and upon it engrave the image of the Serpen -bat which guards the
Gateway of Fire. From the serpent mouth shall issue the tripart Word of Power
that none shall speak or know   .

On the reverse of the Amulet engrave the asterism of Orionis and within the Symbol of
The Hand

On a night when the stars burn in the heavens and the Sun is in the Sign of the Se East
and hold the Amulet aloft saying   :

Great NODENS of the Silver Hand, I call you forth! Behold

the Symbol of your mighty Power!

Open the fiery Gate of your Abode and give life to this

Emblem fashioned by my Art   .

See the Name that may not be spoken,

-Go and turn to the

issue from the jaws of your servant

See the form of your secret place

amongst the stars! I hail you

NODENS !

Stretch out your Hand and lend Power to

my wor

k that the Elder Lords may assist me in

my time of need

. In these Names I call upon your Power

:

BABÃDUR, SHUJÃ, GIBBÕR,

MURZIM , BESN, KLARIA,

GAB BÃRÃ! JABBÃR!

(Make the Elder Sign)

Bow low to each Cardinal Point beginning and ending in the East. Perfume the
Amulet with sweet myrrh of Commiphora, wrap in a black silken cloth and set aside
until you would make use of it

Of The Dead Who Rest Not In Their Tombs & Of Attendant And Familiar Spirits

Where in times past the Old Ones have stained the earth with Their curse, the dead shall know not the peace of the grave. From corruption they shall rise bringing forth a race of ghouls; creatures that

are not of life or death but dwell in the shado

-world of phantasm .

The corpses of evil sorcerers are buried with their faces downwards and their hands spiked with iron to hinder their return to this world. Yet, some with great power yield not to death or the confinement of the sepulchre and by necromantic art, shape the marrow of their backbones to form terrible serpents or great lizards that feed upon noisome remains and gnaw dark passageways to the world of the living .

There are those that rise from the grave at nightfall and drink the blood of man and woman, sometimes transforming into wolf or bat and other diverse shapes   .

The serpen tlike lamia and clawed harpies also spread the plague of torment amongst men as they ever lust for the substance of life that has been denied them .

The worm begets the worm and from the decay of the body strange forms come forth .

The dreams of men and women are sometimes troubled by those passionate spirits of nightmare that the ancients have called incubi and succubi; whereof (through carnal congress) races of halflings are bred .

The wastelands are haunted by Afrit and Jinn, Gorgons and man

-headed Hydras abide with the M - i

Go in the great yellow Desert of the North and my eyes have been infected with their evil

All these beings are easily fascinated and bound to the will of the wizar

-sorcerer who knows the

ways and rites of the Old Ones. But, beware of those who dwell (dead, yet alive) beneath the ancient sands of Egypt (which I learned of in the house of Khephnes) for their time is yet to come and no mortal hand shall stay their power. They shall return

.

Time passes not before the muted idols.

STANZA II .

The Speculum Of Apparitions

To have vision of the conclave of spirits called forth (when not evoked to visible appearance), or commune with the souls of the dead you must prepare a vessel in which their images will be ensnared .

The use of this curious mirror was taught to me by the magicia

-priests of the Vale of ZURNOS

where the Great Night is followed by the Great Day and the Seven Caverns lead to the bowels of the earth .

Take a vessel of crystal glass in the form of the alchemist's retort and set aside. In the day and hour of the Moon (when she is in Her increase) and the Sun in the House of the Scorpion write upon a void parchment the Cypher of the Crab of Zosimos   :

and perfume it with musk   .

In a great mortar mix together: Betony, Pelitory, Snak

-Weed, Elder, Creta

+Dittany of each a like

measure; Zedoary, Galangal, Doronicum, Ammoniac, Opoponax, Spodium, Schaeinanthus, Ebony, Bole-Armenick, Mithridate and Must, each of one third part. Reduce all to a fine powder and put

them within the alchemist's Pelican or blind Alembeck. Add distillate of se

-water to increase the

amalgam fourfold. Cover with the parchment and ferment for the space of

fifteen days. Draw off the Quintessence and fill up the before mentioned retort

with the Elixir and add a

loadstone. Seal up the vessel with red wax and set it on a

brazen tripod. Make the Voorish Sign and speak the Nine

Words of Power   :

LUSOOM, RENGAT, EEPUS,

OMARASY , ALCUM, DARBUS,

NESMONARTIS ,

ENPHODDARIBUISEC, EBO !

At sunset for the space of nine days burn sweet incense beneath the vessel and speak the Words of Power in their order, one upon each day   .

The Apparition of the Spirits shall be seen in the depths of the Speculum when you shall call them by your Art, and the souls of the dead shall give true answer according to their nature

The Visitations Of The Great Old Ones

In metallic stars the Old Ones visit this earth from time to time. And the Lore of the Elder Gods prevails not against this coming; for They walk not the earth in Their forbidden forms

They visit the skies of the desert lands, high places and desolate regions of the earth and strike fear into the heart of the lonely traveller and all who see Their signs. Yet, no man shall divine Their dark purpose or behold Their countenances, for They travel with great swiftness upon the back of the very wind and tear the fabric of Time's web in Their fury

The Beast of Night shall foretell their
coming.

STANZA II I

The Rite Of Transfiguration

Those who would enter the Gulf and yet live must first endure the process of transfiguration. Likewise any that shall continue when the Old Ones return and the earth is cleared off, must take the form of his Masters .

This is the final rite and those who tread this path shall not return to the frame of mortality. His body shall be as iron, his mind shall be one with the oldest and first of earth's Masters; his eyes shall see what no man sees and his shape shall be one with those who walk the dimensions of time

On a night when the eye of the Sta -Ðragon dims and the Sun is in the Fifth House with Saturn in
Trine enter within the Stones and Open the Gate with the Conjuration and Incantation of Yo-g Sothoth. Call forth the Globes by their diverse Names and when They attend you, make upon each coming the Sign of Voor .

Before each of the Stones burn the Incense of Zkauba blowing the Powder of Ibn Ghazi to the Four Winds .

Stand before the Altar facing north and taking the Scimitar of Barzai, trace in the air before you the

three boundary beating Sigils :

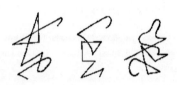

and utter the great Words of Power   :

    RENOSORATUNTA! POHOTHON! BASAKUNNAS   !

In a loud voice call forth the Lord AZATHOTH in

    these words: Great AZATHOTH I call you

    forth!

    Downbreaker of thought

    and form, Come to me

    in Power and clothe m

    e with the Darkness of

    Eternity   !

    Let the Shroud of Nyarlathotep

    descend upon me that I shall walk

    even amongst the star

    and men shall not comprehend

    my presence ZENTO!

    HEDARBUS! TASAC !

    (Make the Sign of Kish)

    Cast this mantle of flesh into the mould of the

    Ancient Ones. I have called you forth !

I have spoken the mighty Words of

your Lore! My father YogSothoth

stands beside the Gate, and Great

Cthulhu calls beneath the waves!

(Make the Sign of Voor)

The thousan dfaced moon has risen !

The Dragon's eye dims! Let yours be opened   !

Trace the Angl eWeb and enter the Gulf by the Formula Dh those without .

-Hna and your form shall be one with

The Augury Of Alhazre d

The words of this book are the venomous thorns that so torture my spirit and my doom is
at hand

The night is filled with Their cries and the beating of leathern wings. Their hand is
at my throat, and though I wear the Triple Talisman upon my breast; the power
wanes with each passing cycle of the Moon.

I dare not sleep the hours from sunset till dawn lest with stealthy skill the Charm is
torn from me and They devour my soul .

The Oracle of Yebsu has foretold of my destruction

when day shall be as night, Their power shall

prevail. A man's life is but a cloud that passes swiftly before the face of the moon.
Yet, there is an Abyss of Perdition where such oblivion is denied, into which my
defiled mind and body shall be cast, to suffer the torments of the damned
throughout the countless ages of infinity, devoid of form or substance .

The Omens are amongst the Stars and grim fear strikes into my bones, my time is at an
end

Yet Al Azif shall not perish for it has passed into the hands of another, a Keeper of Great Powers, who dwells beyond the Western Ocean. Through the ages these writings shall endure, concealed from the many, revealed to the few. In the secrets of my book the wise shall find the Key of Salvation - the fool shall unlock the door to his damnation   .

In the space of nine days hence, the Sun shall join with the Moon and my fate will be sealed

When darkness comes at noon and the sands shiver with the win

I Shall be no more

To the West lies the Cavern of Scrolls,

Where the Brazen Scorpion guards the Forbidden Words.

THE URILIA TEXT

THE following is the Text of URILIA, the Book of the Worm. It contains the formulae by which the wreakers of havoc perform their Rites. These are the prayers of the ensnarers, the liers-in-wait, the blind fiends of Chaos, the most ancient evil.

These incantations are said by the hidden priests and creatures of these powers, defeated by the Elders and the Seven Powers, led by MARDUK, supported by ENKI and the whole Host of IGIGI; defeaters of the Old Serpent, the Ancient Worm, TIAMAT, the ABYSS, also called KUTULU the Corpse-ENKI, yet who lies not dead, but dreaming; he whom secret priests, initiated into the Black Rites, whose names are writ forever in the Book of Chaos, can summon if they but know how.

These words are not to be shown to any man, or the Curse of ENKI are upon thee!

Such are the Words:

IA

IA
IA
IO
IO
IO
I AM the God of Gods
I AM the Lord of Darkness, and Master of Magicians
I AM the Power and the Knowledge
I AM before all things.

I AM before ANU and the IGIGI

I AM before ANU and the ANNUNNAKI
I AM before the Seven SHURUPPAKI
I AM before all things.

I AM before ENKI and SHAMMASH

I AM before all things.

I AM before INANNA and ISHTAR

I AM before NANNA and UDDU
I AM before ENDUKUGGA and NINDUKUGGA
I AM before ERESHKIGAL
I AM before all things.
Before ME was made Nothing that was made.

I AM BEFORE all gods.

I AM before all days.
I AM before all men and legends of men.
I AM the ANCIENT ONE.

NO MAN may seek my resting place.

I receive the Sun at night and the Moon by day.
I AM the reciever of the sacrifice of the Wanderers.
The Mountains of the West cover me.
The Mountains of Magick cover me.

I AM THE ANCIENT OF DAYS.

I AM before ABSU.

I AM before NAR MARRATU.
I AM before ANU.
I AM before KIA.

I AM before all things.

IA! IA! IA! IA SAKKAKTH! IAK SAKKAKH! IA SHA XUL!
IA! IA! IA! UTUKKU XUL!

IA! IA ZIXUL! IA ZIXUL!
IA KINGU! IA AZBUL! IA AZABUA! IA XAZTUR! IA HUBBUR!
IA! IA! IA!
BAXABAXAXAXAXABAXAXAXAXA!
KAKHTAKHTAMON IAS!

II. THE ABOMINATIONS

The terrible offspring of the Ancient Ones may be summoned by the priest. These offspring may be called and adjured to perform what tasks the priest may deem necessary in his temple. They were begotten before all ages and dwelt in the blood of KINGU, and MARDUK could not altogether shut them out. And they dwell in our country, and alongside our generations, though they may not be seen. And this was taught by the priests of Babylon, who charged that these formulae may never be revealed to anyone

who is not initiated into our ways, for to do so would be the most frightful error.

Though they dwell beyond the Gate, they may be summoned when MARDUK is not watchful, and sleeps, on those days when he has no power, when the Great Bear hangs from its tail, and on the four quarters of the year computed therefrom, and on the spaces between these Angles. On these days, the Mother TIAMAT is restless, the corpse KUTULU shakes beneath the Earth, and our Master ENKI is sore afraid.

Prepare, then the bowl of TIAMAT, the DUR of INDUR, the Lost Bowl, the Shattered Bowl of the Sages, summoning thereby the FIRIK of GID, and the Lady SHAKUGUKU, the Queen of the Cauldron. Recite the Conjuration IA ADU EN I over it, and build the Fire therein, calling GBL when thou dost, after his manner and form.

When the Fire is built and conjured, then mayest thou raise thine Dagger, summoning the assistance of NINKHARSAG, Queen of the Demons, and NINKASZI, the Horned Queen, and NINNGHIZHIDDA, the Queen of the Magick Wand, after their manner and form. And when thou hast accomplished this, and made the proper sacrifice, thou mayest begin calling whichsoever of the offspring thou mayest, after opening the Gate.

DO NOT OPEN THE GATE, SAVE FOR AN ESPECIAL TIME THAT THOU STATE AT THE TIME OF OPENING, AND IT MAY NOT STAY OPEN FOR A MOMENT AFTER THE PASSAGE OF THE HOUR OF TIAMAT, ELSE ALL THE ABYSS BREAK FORTH UPON THE EARTH, AND THE DEAD RISE TO EAT THE LIVING, FOR IT IS WRIT: I WILL CAUSE THE DEAD TO RISE AND DEVOUR THE LIVING, I WILL GIVE TO THE DEAD POWER OVER THE LIVING, THAT THEY MAY OUTNUMBER THE LIVING.

After thou hast performed the necessary, called the Spirit, appointed his task, set the time of the closing of the Gate and the return of the Spirit therein, thou must not leave the place of Calling, but remain there until the return of the Spirit and the closing of the Gate.

The Lord of Abominations is HUMWAWA of the South Winds, whose face is a mass of the entrails of the animals and men. His breath is the stench of dung, and has been. HUMWAWA is the Dark Angel of all that is excreted, and of all that sours. And as all things come to the time when they will decay, so also HUMWAWA is the Lord of the Future of all that goes upon the earth, and any man's future years may be seen by gazing into the very face of this Angel, taking care not to breathe the horrid perfume that is the odour of death..

And this is the Signature of HUMWAWA.

And is HUMWAWA appears to the priest, will not the dread PAZUZU also be there? Lord of all fevers and plagues, grinning Dark Angel of the Four Wings, horned, with rotting genitalia, from which he howl in pain through sharpened teeth over the lands of the cities sacred to the APHKHALLU even in the height of the Sun as in the height of the Moon; even with whirling sand and wind, as with empty stillness, and it is the able magician indeed who can remove PAZUZU once he has laid hold of a man, for PAZUZU lays hold unto death.

Know that HUMWAWA and PAZUZU are brothers. HUMAWAW is the eldest, who rides upon a silent, whispering wind and claims the flocks for his own, by which sign you shall know that PAZUZU will come.

And this is the Sigil of PAZUZU by which he is constrained to come:

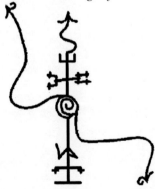

Of all the Gods and Spirits of Abomination, there can be no use or gain to call upon AZAG-THOTH, as he is Surely Mad. Rendered sightless in the Battle, he is Lord of CHAOS, and the priest can find little use for him. He is also too powerful to control once called, and gives violent struggle before sent back to the Gate, for which only a strong and able magician may dare raise him. Thus, for that reason, his seal is not given.

Of all the Gods and Spirits of Abomination, KUTULU only cannot be summoned, for he is the Sleeping Lord. The magician can not hope to have any power over him, but he may be worshipped and for him the proper sacrifices may be made, so that he will spare thee when he rises to the earth. And the times for the sacrifice are the same times as the Sleeping of MARDUK, for this is when Great KUTULU moves. And he is the very Fire of the Earth, and Power of All Magick. When he joins with the Abominations of the Sky, TIAMAT will once more rule the earth!

And this is his Seal:

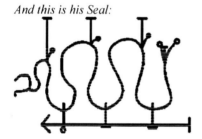

And there are Four Spirits of the Spaces, and they come upon the Wind, and they are Things of the Wind, and of Fire. And the First comes from the North, and is called USTUR, and has a Human Shape. And He is the Most Ancient of the Four, and a Great Lord of the World. And the Second comes from the East, and is called SED and has the Shape of a Bull, but with a human face, and is very mighty. And the Third comes from the south, and is called LAMAS, and is of the Shape of a Lion, but with a human head, and governs those things of the Flame and the Burning Wind. And the Fourth comes from the West, and is called NATTIG, and is of the Shape of an Eagle, but with a human body, having only the face and wings of an Eagle, with an Eagle's claws. And this Eagle comes from the Sea and is a Great Mystery.

And from Nuzku upon Uru they come, and do not wait, and are always present,, and they receive the Wanderers in their Seasons. And the Season of SED is that of the Great Night, when the Bear is slain, and this is in the Month of AIRU. And the Season of LAMAS is the Month of ABU, and that of NATTIG in ARAHSHAMMA and lastly that of USTUR in SHABATU. Thus are the Four Spirits of the Four Spaces, and their Seasons; and they dwell between the Sun's Spaces, and are not of them, but of the Stars, and, as it is said, of the very IGIGI themselves although this is not altogether known.

And to summon these and other Demons, the herb AGLAOPHOTIS must be burnt in a new bowl that must be the Evil Times, and at Night.

And the AKHKHARU may be summoned, which sucketh the blood from a Man, as it desires to become a fashioning of Man, the Blood of KINGU, but the AKHKHARU will never become Man.

And the AKHKHARU may be summoned, if its Sign be known, and it is thus:

And the LALASSU may be called, which haunteth the places of Man, seeking also to become like Man, but these are not to be spoken to, lest the Priest become afflicted with madness, and become unto a living LALASSU which must needs be slain and the Spirit thereof exorcised, for it is Evil and causeth only terror, and no good can come of it. It is like the LALARTU, and of the same Family as that, save the LALARTU was once living and is caught between the Worlds, seeking Entrance into one or the other. And it must not be permitted Entrance into This, for it is of a sickened constitution and will slay mothers at birth, like unto LAMASHTA, the Queen of Sickness and Misery.

And the Signs by which these Things may be summoned are these, if the Priest have need of them, but know that it is not lawful:

And this is the Seal of the LALASSU

And this is the Seal of the LALARTU:

And know that the MINU of ENKI is powerful against these, but against all Operations of Demonic character, and some of these may be rendered fruitless thereby. Therefore it must always be hid.

Know that GELAL and LILIT are quick to come at Calling, and invadeth the beds of Man, robbing the Water of Life and the Food of Life in which to quicken the Dead, but their labours are fruitless for they do not have the formulae. But the Priest has the formulae, and the Food of Life and the Water of Life may be brought to call many, for after the passage of one-tenth of a Moon the Elements are dead.

And GELAL invades the bed of a Woman, and LILIT that of a Man, and sometimes evil beings are born of these hauntings, and as such must be slain, for the children of GELAL are workers natural of the ANCIENT ONE, having His Spirit; and the children of LILIT are likewise, but are born in secret places which may not be perceived by Man, and it is not until the time of their maturity that such as these are given to walking in the places of Men.

And GELAL rideth upon the Wind, but oftentimes LILIT cometh of the Water. Which is why running Water must be used in the Rites, because of the cleanliness thereof.

And the Sign of GELAL is thus:

And the Sign of LILIT is thus:

And XASTUR is a foul demoness who slays Men in their Sleep, and devours that which she will. And of her no more may be said, for it is unlawful; but know that the worshippers of TIAMAT know her well, and that she is beloved of the Ancient Ones.

This is her Sign, by which you may know her:

And know further that the legions of these Evil Ones are uncountable and stretcheth forth on all sides and into all places, though they cannot be seen, except at certain times and to certain persons. And these times are as said before, and the persons unknown, for who can know XASTUR?

But the Dead may be always summoned, and many times are willing to rise; but some are stubborn and desire to remain Where they are, and do not rise, save for the efforts of the Priest, who has power, as ISHTAR, both in this Place and in the Other. And the Dead must be called in the Four Directions, and in the Four Spaces for, not knowing where It is, the Priest must needs take especial care that he call everywhere, for the Spirit may be in flight.

And a Dead God may be also summoned, and the formulae is that which follows. It must be spoken clearly aloud, and not a word changed, else the Spirit of the God may devour thee, as there is no Food and no Drink where they are.

And it must be called in a secret place, without windows, or with windows only in one place, and that should be in the Northern Wall of the place, and the only light shall be of one lamp, set on the altar, and the lamp need not be new, nor the altar, for it is a Rite of

Age and of the Ancient Ones, and they care not for newness.

And the altar should be of a large rock set in the earth, and a sacrifice acceptable unto the nature of the God should be made. And at the time of the Calling, the waters of ABSU will roil, and KUTULU will stir, but unless it be His time, he will not Rise.

And this is the Conjuration of the Dead God:

May NAMMTAR open my eyes that I may see . . . .

May NAMMTAR open my ears that I may hear . . . .
May NAMMTAR open my nose that I may sense His approach.
May NAMMTAR open my mouth that my voice will be heard to the far reaches of the Earth.
May NAMMTAR strengthen my right hand that I shall be strong, to keep the Dead . . . . .

. . . . under my power, under my very power. I
conjure Thee, O Ancestor of the Gods!

I summon Thee, Creature of Darkness, by the Works of Darkness! I
summon Thee, Creature of Hatred, by the Words of Hatred!

I summon Thee, Creature of the Wastes, by the Rites of the Waste!
I summon Thee, Creature of Pain, by the Words of Pain!
I summon and call Thee forth, from Thy Abode in Darkness!
I evoke Thee from Thy resting-place in the bowels of the Earth!
I summon Thine eyes to behold the Brightness of my Wand, which is full of the Fire of
Life!

I conjure Thee, O Ancestor of the Gods!

I summon Thee, Creature of Darkness, by the Works of Darkness! I
summon Thee, Creature of Hatred, by the Works of Hatred!

I summon Thee, Creature of the Wastes, by the Rites of the Waste!
I summon Thee, Creature of Pain, by the Words of Pain!
By the Four Square Pillars of Earth that support the Sky,
May they stand fast against Them that desire to harm me!

I evoke Thee from Thy resting-place in the bowels of the Earth!
I summon Thee and Thine ears to hear the Word that is never spoken, except by Thy
Father, the Eldest of All Who Know Age
The Word that Binds and Commands is my Word!

IA! IA! IA! NNGI BANNA BARRA IA!

IARRUGISHGARRAGNARAB!

I conjure Thee, O Ancestor of the Gods!

I summon Thee, Creature of Darkness, by the Works of Darkness! I
summon Thee, Creature of Hatred, by the Works of Hatred!

I summon Thee, Creature of the Wastes, by the Rites of the Waste!

I summon Thee, Creature of Pain, by the Words of Pain!

I summon Thee, and call Thee forth, from Thy Abode in Darkness!

I evoke Thee from Thy resting-place in the Bowels of the Earth!

MAY THE DEAD RISE!

MAY THE DEAD RISE AND SMELL THE INCENSE!

And this shall be recited only once, and if the God do not appear, do not persist, but finish the Rite quietly, for it means that It hath been summoned elsewhere, or is engaged in some Work which it is better not to disturb.

And when thou hast set out bread for the dead to eat, remember to pour honey thereupon, for it is pleasing to the Goddess Whom No One Worshippeth, Who wanders by night through the streets amid the howling of the dogs and the wailing of the infants, for in Her time a great Temple was built unto Her and sacrifices of infants made that She might save the City from the Enemies who dwelt without. And the Number of infants thus slain is countless and unknowable. And She did save that City, but it was taken soon thereafter when the people no more offered up their children. And when the people made to offer again, at the time of the attack, the Goddess turned her back and fled from her temple, and it is no more. And the Name of the Goddess is no more known. And She maketh the infants restless, and to cry, so the reason for the pouring of honey over the sacred bread, for it is written:

Bread of the Cult of the Dead in its Place I eat

In the Court prepared
Water of the Cult of the Dead in its Place I drink
A Queen am I, Who has become estranged to the Cities
She that comes from the Lowlands in a sunken boat
Am I.

I AM THE VIRGIN GODDESS

HOSTILE TO MY CITY
A STRANGER IN MY STREETS.
MUSIGAMENNA URUMA BUR ME YENSULAMU
GIRME EN!
Oh, Spirit, who understand thee? Who comprehend Thee?

Now, there are Two Incantation to the Ancient Ones set down here, which are well known to the Sorcerers of the Night, they who make images and burn them by the Moon and by other Things. And they burn them by the Moon and by other Things. And they

burn unlawful grasses and herbs, and raise tremendous Evils, and their Words are never written down, it is said. But there are. And they are Prayers of Emptiness and Darkness, which rob the Spirit.

Hymn To the Ancient Ones

They are lying down, the Great Old Ones.

The bolts are fallen and the fastenings are placed.
The crowds are quiet and the people are quiet.
The Elder Gods of the Land
The Elder Goddesses of the Land
SHAMMASH
SIN
ADAD
ISHTAR
Have gone to sleep in heaven.
They are not pronouncing judgements.
They are no deciding decisions.
Veiled is the Night.
The Temple and the Most Holy Places are quiet and dark.
The Judge of Truth
The Father of the Fatherless
SHAMMASH
Has gone to his chamber.
O Ancient Ones!
Gods of the Night!
AZABUA!

IAK SAKKAK!
KUTULU!
NINNGHIZHIDDA!
O Bright One, GIBIL!
O Warrior, IRRA!
Seven Stars of Seven Powers!
Ever-Shining Star of the North!
SIRIUS!
DRACONIS!
CAPRICORNUS!
Stand by and accept
This sacrifice I offer
May it be acceptable
To the Most Ancient Gods!

IA MASHMASHTI! KAKAMMU SELAH!

Invocation of the Powers

Spirit of the Earth, Remember!

Spirit of the Seas, Remember!
In the Names of the Most Secret Spirits of NAR MARRATUK
The Sea below the seas
And of KUTULU
The Serpent who sleepeth Dead
From beyond the graves of the Kings
From beyond the tomb wherein INANNA
Daughter of the Gods
Gained Entrance to the Unholy Slumbers
Of the she-fiend of KUTHULETH

In SHURRUPAK, I summon thee to mine aid!

In UR, I summon thee to mine aid!
In NIPPURR, I summon thee to mine aid!
In ERIDU, I summon thee to mine aid!
In KULLAH, I summon thee to mine aid!
In LAAGASH, I summon thee to mine aid!
Rise up, O powers from the Sea below all seas
From the grave beyond all graves
From the Land of TIL
To SHIN
NEBO
ISHTAR
SHAMMASH
NERGAL
MARDUK
ADAR

House of the Water of Life

Pale ENNKIDU
Hear me!

Spirit of the Seas, Remember!

Spirit of the Graves, Remember!

And with these incantations, and with others, the sorcerers and the she-sorcerers call many things that harm of the life of man. And they fashion images out of wax, and out of flour and honey, and of all the metals, and burn them or otherwise destroy them, and chant the civilisations. And they cause plagues, for they summon PAZUZU. And they cause madness, for they call AZAGTHOTH. And these Spirits come upon the Wind, and some upon the Earth, crawling. And no oil, no powder, suffices to save a man from this

inquity, save that exorcisms handed down and recited by the able Priest. And they work by the Moon, and not by the Sun, and by older planets than the Chaldaens were aware. And in cords, they tie knows, and each is a spell. And if these knots be found, they may be untied, and the cords burnt, and the spell shall be broken, as it is written:

AND THEIR SORCERIES SHALL BE AS MOLTEN WAX, AND NO MORE.

And a man may cry out, what have I don't, and my generation that such evil shall befall me? And it mean nothing, save that a man, being born, is of sadness, for he is of the Blood of the Ancient Ones, but has the Spirit of the Elder Gods breathed into him. And his body goes to the Ancient Ones, but his mind is turned towards the Elder Gods, and this is the War which shall be always fought, unto the last generation of man; for the World is unnatural. When the Great KUTULU rises up and greets the Stars, then the War will be over, and the World be One.

Such is the Covenant of the Abominations and the End of this Text.

BOOK OF NYARLATHOTEP

NYARLATHOTEP
PRIMUM

This is the book of the laws and practices of the sleeping dead, written by myself, Abd Al-Hazred - the great sorcerer and poet. With the secrets in this book I have spoken with dark spirits, who have furnished me with many riches, both in the form of money and knowledge, I have even learned the unlearnable knowledge of the divine ones, such is the
power of what I learned. I have also learned of the Old Spirits, who lived before man, and still live dreaming, and they are very terrible. It was a face of one of these very spirits that initiated me into this powerful magic.

One morning I awoke to see that the world had changed, the sky was darker and rumbled with the voices of evil spirits and flowers and life had been strangled by them also. Then I heard the screaming call, the screaming of something beyond the hills which was calling me. The screaming call maddened me and made me sweat, in the end I could not ignore it and decided to find what manner of beast was making the screaming call. I left my house and set out into the desert with the call sounding all around me. In the desert I wandered, without anything but the clothes that I was wearing, I sweated during the day and froze during the night. But still the screaming call kept on.

On the third day, on the eighteenth hour of that day, the screaming call stopped and standing in front of me was a man. The man was completely black, both in face and clothing, and he greeted me in my tongue and with my name. The man told me his name and his name was Ebonor and he was a demon. Ebonor was the one who had made the screaming call and I did not yet know that he was more than the lesser demon that torments the infirm, he was the messenger of the most evil spirits called the Old Spirits, which even the most powerful sorcerer of even God cannot completely control. This demon gave me the gift to understand all languages, whether it be written or spoken or of man or beast. This is why I, Abd Al-Hazred, have been able to read documents which have confused many lesser mortals for many decades, but I have also been able never to get peace. For even when I try to lay down and sleep, I can hear the creatures around me speaking, I can hear the birds and the desert insects, but worst of all the dogs, which madly growl and bark about the coming of the Old Spirits.

Now that the screaming call had ceased, I returned to my town with my new knowledge and had many sleepless nights, listening to the sound of the smallest beast and invisible demons talking, only where everything is dead could I ever sleep, thought I.

After many days without sleep I set out into the desert once more, hoping to find Ebonor and to make him take back his gift, for I had found it to be a most terrible curse. For three days and eighteen hours I wandered again and on the eighteenth hour Ebonor appeared to me. I fell before him and begged him to take back his gift as it was driving my mind away from me, but he did not show any compassion. Instead he said that he would show me more knowledge. He took my hand and led me beneath the cold desert sands, down many sets of steps, untrod by man, until we reached the door to a secret chamber. In here, you shall find the ultimate truths, but you shall only understand a little, said the demon to

me as he opened the door. Then I heard the screaming call coming from the portal, but this time it was a thousand times more intense and Ebonor took my hand and pulled me across the threshold. Through that door I saw all the untold knowledge, although only a little has my mind retained.

And when the learning was at an end, I found myself back in the desert standing by Ebonor, who laughed at me and jested that the mind of man was much inferior to that of the Old Spirits. I had learned of the Old Spirits in the secret chamber, they were most terrible and evil spirits who came from outside creation to live upon the earth. Then at a time before man was born they were expelled from the earth because the stars became wrong. All were expelled from the earth except for Nyarlathotep, the dark one or Egypt and the messenger of the Old Spirits, of which Ebonor was one face. Turning away from me, Ebonor laughed again and said to me that one day a time will come when the stars are right again and the Old Spirits shall return. With this having been said, I was alone once more.

I decided to rest, although my cursed gift was still with me. It was when I rested that I realised that I was holding a book, the book contained the many names of Nyarlathotep, the Old Spirit's messenger. I was able to read this book perfectly, but no one else was able to, for they said that they could not understand the words on the pages. The book told me that Nyarlathotep has twenty-one names, or faces. Each of these names may be called upon in their correct hours, from the third hour in the day to the penultimate hour in the day. With each name is a sacred and special sign, which must also be used with the correct invocation. The names of Nyarlathotep are thus;

The name of the third hour is Etonetatae and he is master of magical words and phrases and he should be consulted much in your work, for he will deliver to you many words of power. Etonetatae has no body, but may manifest as a mist or may remain invisible.

The name of the fourth hour is Odanen, who brings with him the wishes of the Old Spirits, you may wish to communicate with Odanen, rather than with the Old Spirits themselves, for it is many times safer. Odanen will appear before the magician as a shadowy figure who is only just visible.

The name of the fifth hour is Banibo, who will reveal to the magician the whereabouts of splendid treasures, but be warned - do not let him persuade you to leave your circle, be sure to get the directions from him and then banish him. Banibo appears as a deformed and bloated man and emanated the odour of rotting matter.

The name of the sixth hour is Obinab, who will reveal to the magician many secrets concerning the universe. He is Banibo's opposite, but he will still urge you to leave the circle so that he may take you on a journey. If he does this then insist that he himself gives you the knowledge which would be attained from the journey.

The name of the seventh hour is Bosoro, who will appear as a huge and fiery snake - do not look into it's eyes or you shall be trapped forever, but command him to appear in human form and he will have to obey. Bosoro has the knowledge of men's minds and you may ask him to reveal the knowledge of a man which you shall name.

The name of the eighth hour is Oxeren, who has knowledge of the future and will appear on a black horse, which can run faster than time itself.

The name of the ninth hour is Badero, who is the lord of gestures and will teach the conjurer many magical gestures, with which he shall be able to open gates to other places or effect the minds of men.

The name of the tenth hour is Osenin, who has control over the bodies of men and can change a man into any shape the magician tells him. Osenin appears with the body of a man and the head of a lizard, which is enveloped in flame.

The name of the eleventh hour is Boxebo, who will make doors open for the magician so that his way is not restricted. Boxebo appears as a huge insect with many pairs of hands.

The name of the twelfth hour is Norano, who knows of all the books which have ever existed and she will dictate to the magician whichever book he seeks at that time. Norano appears as a winged scribe.

The name of the thirteenth hour is Onaron, who has much knowledge of the sciences which he will tell to the magician and he may even be commanded to bring to the magician rare materials, such as herbs and stones. Onaron appears a winged man with many long and sharp teeth.

The name of the fourteenth hour is Nerexo, who holds information about secret talismen and seals. Nerexo appears in the form of an old man with the legs of a goat.

The name of the fifteenth hour is Reranber, who is a most evil spirit and will murder any man at your command. Reranber will appear as a prince in shimmering gold holding a black sword.

The name of the sixteenth hour is Orosob, who is a most lustful demon and will procure any woman that the magician wishes. Orosob appears as an unclothed black man and if he does not appear it is because he is walking the land ravishing the unwary, so you should call him again, but do not call him more than three times or you shall enrage him.

The name of the seventeenth hour is Nineso, who will appear exactly like the magician. Nineso has the power to conjure many lesser spirits and the magician should command him which spirits he should conjure.

The name of the eighteenth hour is Ebonor, who will reveal the knowledge that is not of man and also understands all languages. The magician should question him and should not urge him to give the gifts of knowledge and language, as he gave to me - for to do so would anger him. Ebonor will appear as a black man, clothed in a black robe.

The name of the nineteenth hour is Oredab, who appears as a skeleton riding atop a great lizard. Oredab has the power to destroy whole cities in one gesture.

The name of the twentieth hour is Nenado who has much strength and can effect the movement of the stars and planets. Nenando will appear with the body of a statue and the head of a fly larvae.

The name of the twenty-first hour is Rubanir, who's appearance changes constantly and will always be unidentifiable. Rubanir has knowledge of all things past.

The name of the twenty-second hour is Obexob, who appears as the floating corpse of a pharaoh enveloped in flames. Obexob will deliver visions to the magician who studies the   flames closely.

The name of the twenty-third hour is Etananesoe, who is too terrible to behold. Etananesoe is the true incarnation of Nyarlathotep and will only appear at the time when   the stars are right for himself.

Those are the twenty-one names of Nyarlathotep and the name may be summoned at the appropriate hour using the conjurations which I shall set down later in my writing, be warned though - do not summon more than one face in a day, otherwise Nyarlathotep will become enraged and break the circle, devouring the magician.

With the book containing this knowledge, I set about seeking a new abode, for I could not return to my village, for I needed time to study the ways of the Old Spirits and I needed a dead place, so that I could sleep undisturbed. After many days of walking I eventually   found myself at the cavernous ruins of a city, which was once called Ubar, this was   where I decided to dwell. In my solitude I was able to practice my art and learned much from the names of Nyarlathotep and I even dared to conjure some of the Old Spirits, with very grave consequences, for I was not prepared for the destruction they would cause - for no circle can hold them. I also wrote down all that I learned that was writeable so that this knowledge may be passed on and shall not be lost again.

NYARLATHOTEP
SECUNDUM

In this chapter I shall reveal the names, natures and seals of the Old Spirits. Once the Old   Spirits lived on the earth, but when the stars changed they were expelled and separated.   There are, however, times when the stars become right for certain spirits and these are the times which they can be summoned on. There are forty-five Old Spirits who are very terrible and very powerful, for this reason I ask you never to summon them apart from in exceptional situations. If you do risk summoning then almost certain death shall await if you have not made the appropriate preparations - for they cannot be banished easily and will inflict terrible damage once summoned. The stars become right for the Old Spirits as the zodiac's band travels across the heavens and the times upon which they may be conjured upon shall now be revealed.

Starting seven degrees from the Archer's sign and proceeding deosil, I shall work my way around the wheel of the zodiac, explaining when the stars are right for each of the Old Spirits.

In the seventh to the thirteenth degrees the stars are right for Uk-Han, who appears as a huge, horned snake.

In the fourteenth to twentieth degrees the stars are right for Magoth, who appears like a large and strange cat creature with the tentacles of a squid on it's front.

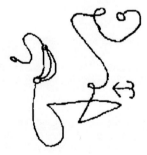

In the twenty-first to twenty-seventh degrees the stars are right for Yak-Ishath, which appears as something too terrible to behold - an ever changing mass featuring the faces of the souls it has swallowed.

In the twenty-eighth to thirty-fourth degrees the stars are right for Lunigguroth, who appears as a sphere of glowing white, from which vast multitudes of horrors pour.

In the thirty-fifth to forty-first degrees the stars are right for Tursoth, who appears as a giant scale covered man with the legs of a spider.

In the forty-second to forty-eight degrees the stars are right for Marbel, who has no body, but the sound will be most apparent, causing ears to bleed and animals to fall down dead.

In the forty-ninth to fifty-fifth degrees the stars are right for Diabaka, who appears as a huge, flaming monstrosity, surrounded by fiery suns.

In the fifty-sixth to sixty-second degrees, nothing may be summoned, not even the lesser faces of Nyarlathotep, for this is a time when the stars are wrong for every denomination of Old Spirit.

In the sixty-third to sixty-ninth degrees the stars are right for Cthuhanai, who appears as a great winged man with the head of a decaying lizard bird.

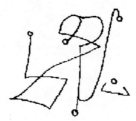

In the seventieth to seventy-sixth degrees the stars are right for Nagoango, who shall appear from the ground and try to swallow you whole.

In the seventy-seventh to eighty-third degrees the stars are right for Vagonch, who will appear as a huge mass of whiteness which will swallow anything which comes near.

In the eighty-fourth to ninetieth degrees the stars are right for Pul-Marg, who shall appear as a black demon with the power to petrify the people who's gaze he catches.

In the ninety-first to ninety-seventh degrees the stars are right for Bovadoit, who cannot be summoned because of her size and terribleness. Bovadoit shall be locked out until the stars are fully right.

In the ninety-eight to one-hundred and fourth degrees the stars are right for Parahan, who shall appear as a great dragon, but with a small, many eyed head.

During the one-hundred and fifth to the one-hundred and eleventh degrees, nothing may be conjured.

In the one-hundred and twelfth to one-hundred and eighteenth degrees the stars are right for Yurnal, which shall appear as a great gray and lumbering thing, too vast for the eye to view.

During the one-hundred and nineteenth to the one-hundred and twenty-fifth degrees, nothing may be summoned.

In the one-hundred and twenty-sixth to one-hundred and thirty-second degrees the stars are right for Cthulhu, who appears as a great man with dragon's wings and an octopus' head.

During the one-hundred and thirty-third to one-hundred and thirty-ninth degrees there must be not conjuration.

In the one-hundred and fortieth to one-hundred and forty-sixth degrees the stars are right for Nersel, who appears as an enraged ghoul and is ruler of Zin.

In the one-hundred and forty-seventh to one-hundred and fifty-third degrees the stars are right of Andryn, who is the weakest of the Old Spirits as he cannot harm the holder of the second ring of Nerexo. If Andryn attacks the magician, he should kiss the ring and speak the word "OROGOT".

In the one-hundred and fifty-fourth to one-hundred and sixtieth degrees the stars are right for Unspeterus, who appears like a huge black toad.

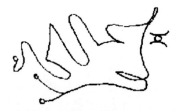

In the one-hundred and sixty-first to one-hundred and sixty-seventh degrees the stars are right for Bas-Juob, who appears like a great slimy maggot with the tentacles of a sea dragon.

In the one-hundred and sixty-eight to one-hundred and sevent-fourth degrees the stars are right for Astursoth, who appears as a great moaning mass, the sounds which echo from it's heart are enough to make men fall and die.

In the one-hundred and seventy-fifth to one-hundred and eighty-first degrees the stars are right for Azalu, who appears as a great plant beast with many arms and heads.

In the one-hundred and eighty-second to one-hundred and eighty-eight degrees the stars are right for Leasynoth, who appears like a great dragon and worm, who lived beneath the mountains in the time of the Old Spirits ruling.

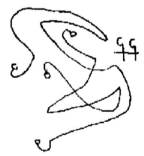

In the one-hundred and eighty-ninth to one-hundred and ninety-fifth degrees the stars are right for Yog-Thothai, who appears like a huge, screaming bat with crawling worms for a face. Yog-Thothai can travel far away, sometimes carrying prey to distant stars.

In the one-hundred and ninety-sixth to two-hundred and second degrees the stars are right for Maphleus, who appears as a huge shapeless form which can divide into many smaller forms.

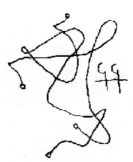

In the two-hundred and third to two-hundred and ninth degrees, the stars are right for Nun-Hanish and her brood, who appear as a whole army of ghouls, which may travel into   men's dreams.

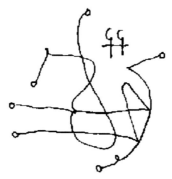

In the two-hundred and tenth to two-hundred and sixteenth degrees the stars are right for Bas-Lesifa, who appears as a dark orb which cannot be harmed and spreads a plague of madness all around.

In the two-hundred and seventeenth to two-hundred and twenty-third degrees the stars are right for Mememyet-Raha and her children, who appear as vast and slimy horned beasts.

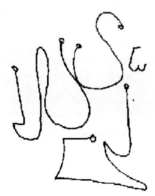

During the two-hundred and twenty-fourth to two-hundred and twenty-eighth degrees the stars are most wrong and no evocation may take place.

In the two-hundred and thirty-ninth to two-hundred and forty-fourth degrees the stars are right for Azathoth, who appeareth as a vast and shapeless form of screaming souls and he will be most angry at being drawn away from his secret space.

In the two-hundred and forty-fifth to two-hundred and fifty-first degrees the stars are right for Paturnigish, who appears as a great cloud.

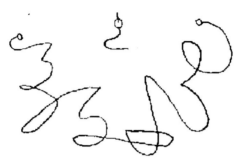

In the two-hundred and fifty-second to two-hundred and fifty-eigth degrees the stars are right for Dagaon, who appears as a gigantic man with the face of a long toothed fish.

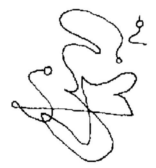

In the two-hundred and fifty-ninth to two-hundred and sixty-fifth degrees the stars are right for Ayam, who appears like a great tree made of flesh.

In the two-hundred and sixty-sixth to two-hundred and seventy-second degrees the stars are right for Etananesoe, the true face of Nyarlathotep.

In the two-hundred and seventy-third to two-hundred and seventy-ninth degrees the stars are right for Bugg, who appears like a great furry snake man.

In the two-hundred and eightieth to two-hundred and eighty-sixth degrees the stars are right for Yog-Sothoth, who appears like a great nothingness, a gate which leads outside onto the surface of his vast body.

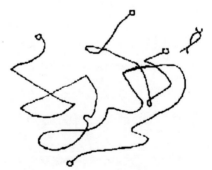

During the two-hundred and eighty-seventh to the two-hundred and ninety-third degrees no conjurations may take place.

In the two-hundred and ninety-fourth to three-hundredth degrees the stars are right for Moivoo, who appears in a form so complex that no man can describe him.

In the three-hundred and first to three-hundred and seventh degrees the stars are right for Beeluge, who appears like a huge lizard with the mouth of an insect.

In the three-hundred and eighth to three-hundred and fourteenth degrees the stars are right for Caim, who appears like a hissing spider thing.

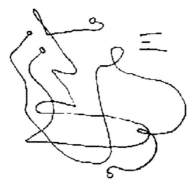

In the three-hundredth and fifteenth to three-hundred and twenty-first degrees the stars are right for Lusoath, who appears like a great cone of crystal, which no man should touch, or else his mind be stolen away.

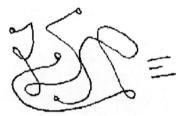

In the three-hundred and twenty-second to three-hundred and twenty-eigth degrees the stars are right for Lusoath, who appears like a great walking mass of earth.

In the three-hundred and twenty-ninth to three-hundred and thirty-fifth degrees the stars are right for Tsapetae, who appears like a great swirling darkness.

In the three-hundred and thirty-sixth to three-hundred and forty-second degrees the stars are right for Nun-Buhan, who will appear all around the magician like a great horde of worms.

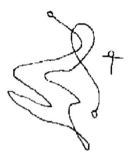

In the three-hundred and forty-third to three-hundred and forty-ninth degrees the stars are right for Hasariel, who will appear like a large flying fiend.

In the three-hundred and fiftieth to three-hundred and fifty-sixth degrees the stars are right for Carr-Vephat, who will appear like a vast mass with dark globes circling all around.

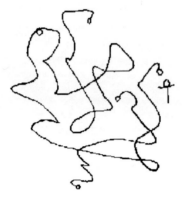

In the three-hundred and fifty-seventh to third degrees the star are right for Detathit, who appears like a river of grabbing hands and dragon's heads.

During the fourth to sixth degrees there must be no conjuration and you must carry out the Great Banishing ritual.

Now that you know their times, names and seals I shall once more urge you never to summon any of them except in very exceptional and important situations - if you are a ruler than I tell you never to summon them for battle, or else chaos will ensure. If you are curious I tell you never to summon them to satisfy that curiosity or much terror and death will come of it. If you would manipulate them to bring you your desired then summon them not, but instead conjure a name of Nyarlathotep, for the Old Sprits will not heed your desires because they have no masters. You must also know that there is no way to banish the Old Spirits, they shall only depart when the stars change and become wrong for them.

NYARLATHOTEP
TERTIUM

In this book I shall explain the creation of the magical tools that the magician will need to summon the spirits which I have told of in the last two chapters. Take care to construct the tools exactly as I tell you and as I have been told by the names of the hours, for if you do not then they will hold no power. I know of the tools for the lesser conjurations, those of the names of the hours, and I know of the tools which the magician shall use to conjure the Old Spirits - but I only know a few methods of protection against the Old Spirits. For this reason I pray that you will summon the names of Etonetatae, Badero and Nerexo and command them to speak truly to you and to tell you of any protective devices which are available against the Old Spirit which you seek to conjure.

In all matters of conjuration you will need the cardinal tools of the wand, the knife, the perfume, the fire and the parchments. When one would conjure the Old Spirits you will also need the sword, the stones and the ring. Additional to all these things the magician must be wearing the appropriate clothing, which bears the appropriate seals and signs.

Firstly the robe is to be made of black material and should be a hooded garment. The robe is to be a new robe made of the magician's hand and should never be used for anything but the work - else it will be spoiled. Starting upon the first day of the week you must do the following - In the hour of Venus you should make the final stitch in the garment and keep it hidden until the next day. On the next day, in the hour of Mercury you should create the following seal on the left arm of the garment and keep it hidden until the next day.

On the next day, in the hour of the Moon you should create the following seal on the right arm of the garment and keep it hidden until the next day.

On the next day, in the hour of Saturn you should create the following seal on the genital area of the garment and keep it hidden until the next day.

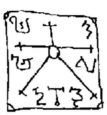

On the next day, in the hour of Jupiter you should create the following seal on the back of the garment and keep it hidden until the next day.

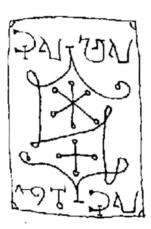

On the next day, in the hour of Mars you should create the following seal on the front of the garment and keep it hidden until the next day. Take care to reproduce it exactly as it appears, for this is the most important of the seals which you will make on the garment.

On the final day, in the hour of the Sun, take the robe from it's resting place. Before you continue check it for any imperfections in the patterns and once you are sure of their perfection you may commence with the consecration of the robe. For all of the tools which are concerned with the lesser conjurings, you shall use the following consecration, but for the tools which will only be used to conjure the Old Spirits you shall use a later consecration. The consecration is thus; You shall take boughs of laurel and build a fire, which you shall light as the hour in which you commenced the work is quarter through. Now, before the fire, with the tool in your hands, above the flames, not so low that it shall

burn or be damaged and not so high that it will not be touched by the smoke. you shall speak the following:

Samak daram surabel karameka

amuranas Ekotos mirat-fortin

ranerug Dalerinter marban porafin

Herikoramonus derogex

Iratisinger

I call thee, O mighty names of the

hours, The faces of the faceless

Nyarlathotep, That you may become

one in this hour, To watch my art be

done,

That you will grant this tool which I have

fashioned, The power that it is right to have,

For I have created it in the image of

perfection, And it cannot be undone,

Iratisinger

Herikoramonus derogex

Dalerinter marban porafin

Ekotos mirat-fortin ranerug

Samak daram surabel karameka amuranas

Sedhi!

Ihdes!

In the all binding name of Nyarlathotep,

Give power this tool,

Give power.

Doros serod!

This conjuration shall be comitted to memory, and shall always be done without book
or parchment. Where in this conjuration and where throughout the remainder of the
book I write + this shall be the signal for the conjurer to make the sign that gains the
attention of the names of the Nyarlathotep and aids them in their coming. This sign is
simple and shall be done with the left hand. You should touch your forehead with two
of your fingers, then you should draw them down to the chest and touch the heart.
Then the fingers should touch the left shoulder, the forehead once more and then the
right shoulder.

Now that the robe has been made you shall fashion the wand. In the day following the construction of the robe, in the hour of Venus, you should cut the branch of a cypress tree and carve it into a smooth wand, being just over one foot in length. You should also be wearing your robe during the construction of the tools and you shall keep all of your tools wrapped in the robe, which you shall keep hidden. Having carved the wand on the next day you shall take a knife which is pure and has hurt no-one and in the hour of Mercury shall write these signs on the knife:

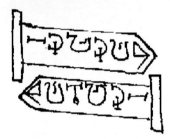

Then in that same hour you shall consecrate the dagger and place it in the fire that it shall be cleansed. On the day that follows, in the hour of the Moon, you shall engrave the sign of Ekotos on the wand. The sign should be engraved four times along the length of the wand, the wand should then be turned to the next quarter and the sign engraved four more times. Repeat this until you have come full circle and the wand has sixteen representations of the seal upon it, which is thus:

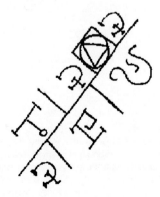

Then, at the top of the wand make the ring of Mirat-Fortin, which is thus:

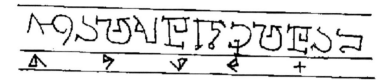

On the day that follows, in the hour of Saturn, you shall consecrate the wand.

Now the perfume should be made and you shall always make it on Monday, in the Moons hour and you shall always consecrate it halfway through the Moon's hour on the day in which you have made it. You should take equal parts of mint, frankincense, wormwood, sage, sandalwood, storax and musk, which you will mix together and create a powder from. This powder shall be kept in a bottle which is purple in colour and has the following seal inscribed on it's stopper, which shall be made of iron:

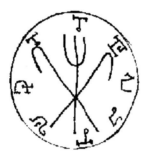

The fire shall be constructed before any act of conjuration takes place and shall be left to burn at the north of the circle for quarter of an hour before the conjuration takes place. It should be made of laurel and cypress wood and once lit, you should say the blessing. If you have not built a circle then one should be made one hour before the conjuration takes place and it can then be left there permenently or erased. For the lesser conjurations a circle made of flour, chalked upon a floor, or cut into the earth will suffice, however, for the greater conjurations, those of the Old Spirits, the circle should be cut into the ground and then filled in with a mixture flour and silver - else the conjurer shall surely die.
Having built the circle the conjurer must make the blessing. If he seeks to conjure a name of Nyarlathotep then the conjuration which has been used for the other items shall suffice. If the conjurer seeks to summon the Old Spirits then the Great Consecration should be made, which will follow later in this book.

The final tool which you will require for the lesser conjurations are the parchments, upon which you shall write any conjurations and subjugations which you shall need during the work. The parchments should be written in the day before the work will take place at the hour at which it shall take place on the next day. You shall write upon pure, virgin parchment with ink that has been consecrated for the conjuration in question.

If the magician would seek to conjure the Old Spirits, then he shall need several additional tools. The first tool is the sword, which like the dagger shall not have harmed any person or animal. Take this sword in the hour of Mercury and upon the sword engrave the following signs:

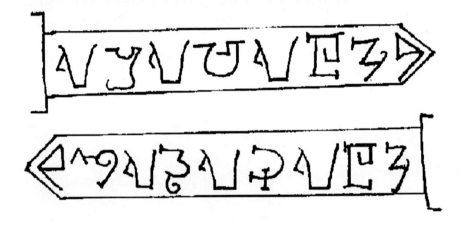

The tools which you shall need in conjuring the Old Spirits shall be kept separate from those used in the lesser conjurations and each shall be wrapped in dark green silk, upon which the seal of Unity has been sewn and it is thus:

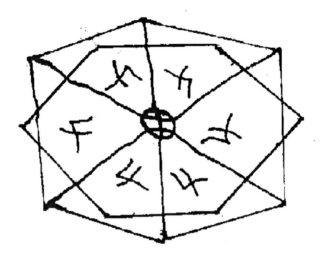

The sword should be wrapped in this silk and kept hidden. For the space of one moon, each night in the hour of Mercury you shall pray infront of the sword, which you shall keep wrapped in the cover. And you shall pray thus:

Samak daram surabel karameka

amuranas Ekotos mirat-fortin

ranerug Dalerinter marban porafin

Herikoramonus derogex

Iratisinger

Axarath Malakath

Axarath Malakath

Iratisinger

Herikoramonus derogex

+Dalerinter marban

porafin

Ekotos mirat-fortin ranerug

Samak daram surabel karameka amuranas

Sedhi!

Ihdes!

This is the prayer of the Great Consecration and you should commit it into memory as with the consecration which has gone before. After the space of one moon has passed you shall take the sword and in the hour of Mercury you shall make a fire. You shall then anoint the sword with the perfume, which has been mixed in part with water. Then you shall hold the sword above the fire at the same hight as before - not so it is in the flames and not so that the smoke cannot touch it. Then you shall pronounce the Great Consecration, which is thus:

Samak daram surabel karameka

amuranas Ekotos mirat-fortin

ranerug Dalerinter marban porafin

Herikoramonus derogex

Iratisinger

Axarath Malakath

I call thee, O spirits of the starry

band, I call thee, O Old Spirits,

I call thee from your places or

rest That you may come unto

me, And watch my art be done,

In your names I have fashioned this tool,

And in your names I shall pledge it,+

By your powers I pray that you will grant the
tool

The power that it is right to have,

In the names of

Uk-Han,

Tursoth,

Cthuhanai,

Bovadoit,

Cthulhu,

Unspeterus,

Leasynoth,

Mememyet-Raha,

Paturnigish,

Bugg,

Beeluge,

Nun-

Buhan,

I command thee to consecrate this tool,

For I have created it in the image of

perfection,

And it cannot be undone,

Axarath Malakath

Iratisinger

Herikoramonus derogex

Dalerinter marban porafin

Ekotos mirat-fortin ranerug

Samak daram surabel karameka amuranas

Sedhi!

Ihdes!

In the all binding name of Mirat-Fortin,

Give power this tool,

Give power.

Doros serod!

The Great Consecration shall also be memorised by the magician. Upon finishing the great conescration you shall place the sword into the fire that it may be consecrated in the name of the Old Spirits. When the fire has consumed itself you shall leave the sword to become cold once more and then place it in it's cover where it shall remain hidden until it is called for.

Next you shall make the stones, which shall be used to mark the circle when you would conjure the Old Spirits, for it pleases them. You should take twelve stones and they shall all be like to the size of your fist and the stones which you collect shall be Lapis Lazuli, Amber, Onyx, Bloodstone, Agate, Obsidian, Turquoise, Topaz, Coral, Jet, Quartz and Jade. You shall keep these stones wrapped in a similar covering to the sword and shall keep them hidden. You shall also cite the prayer of the Great Consecration for the cycle of one moon as with the sword, but this shall be done in the hour of the Moon. After the course of one moon you shall perform the Great Consecration upon each stone, having first engraved them with the appropriate signs. Upon the stone of Lapis Lazuli engrave the sign which I have placed next to the seals for the Spirits who may be conjured between seven and thirty-fourth degrees. Upon the stone of Amber engrave the sign which I have placed next to the seals of the Spirits who may be conjured between thirty- five and sixty-two degrees. Upon the stone of Onyx engrave the sign which I have placed next to the seals of the Spirits who may be conjured between sixty-three and ninety degrees. Upon the Bloodstone engrave the sign which I have placed next to the seals of the Spirits who may be conjured between ninety-one and and one-hundred and twenty- five degrees. Upon the stone of Agate engrave the sign which I have placed next to the seals of the Spirits who may be conjured between one-hundred and twenty-six and one- hundred and fifty-three degrees. Upon the stone of Obsidian engrave the sign which I have placed next to the seals of the Spirits who may be conjured between one-hundred and fifty-four and one-hundred and eighty-one degrees. Upon the stone of Turquoise engrave the sign which I have placed next to the seals of the Spirits who may be conjured between one-hundred and eighty-two and two-hundred and sixteen degrees. Upon the stone of Topaz engrave the sign which I have placed next to the seals of the Spirits who may be conjured between two-hundred and seventeen and two-hundred and forty-four degrees. Upon the Coral engrave the sign which I have placed next to the seals of the Spirits who may be conjured between two-hundred and forty-five and two-hundred and seventy-two degrees. Upon the stone of Jet engrave the sign which I have placed next to

the seals of the Spirits who may be conjured between two-hundred and seventy-three and three-hundred degrees. Upon the stone of Quartz engrave the sign which I have placed next to the seals of the Spirits who may be conjured between three-hundred and one and three-hundred and thirty-five degrees. Upon the stone of Jade engrave the sign which I have placed next to the seals of the Spirits who may be conjured between three-hundred and thirty-six and three degrees. After each stone is consecrated place it upon the cover which the seal of Unity has been made upon. You shall consecrate them in the order which I have written them above and once more keep them hidden until the time of their use is at hand.

The final tool which shall be required is the ring, which shall offer some small protection to the magician who would conjure the Old Spirits, though the protection may be small it would certainly be most foolish to attempt to summon the Old Ones without it. The ring of gold and disc of silver shall be forged in the hour of Saturn and kept hidden, wrapped in green silk upon which the seal of Unity has been made. In the hour of Saturn, on the day that follows the forging of the ring, you shall engrave these characters upon the ring:

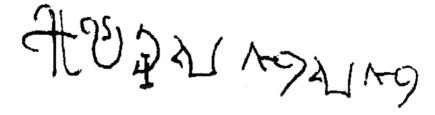

And upon the disc you shall engrave these characters:

Once more, for the space of one moon you shall keep the ring wrapped and pray the prayer of the Great Consecration before it. When the moon has made it's cycle you shall perform the Great Consecration in the hour of Saturn, having first anointed the ring with a mixture made from the perfume, flour and water. As with the sword, the ring shall be cast into the fire once the Great Consecration has come to an end. Now that the ring has been created, should you feel the Old Spirits attempt to penetrate the circle you shall kiss the ring and say "ABROSAX", for this will strengthen the circle for a small time. But you must remember that there is no permenant protection from them and they will break through the circle in a short time whatever protection you may have.

NYARLATHOTEP
QUARTUM

This book will give the magician instruction on how he shall create the circle. As I have said before, the circle should be made strong enough to hold out the spirits for the duration of the conjuration. Should you seek to conjure on of the many faces of Nyarlathotep then the circle may be made from flour, chalk or cut into the earth with the knife or sword. If you would seek to conjure the Greater Spirits then the circle must be cut into the earth or into stone and then it must be filled in with flour and silver dust, for silver offers most excellent protection against the spirits, as does the stone Kinocetus, which may also be powdered for the purpose of strengthening the circle. The form of the circle is thus;

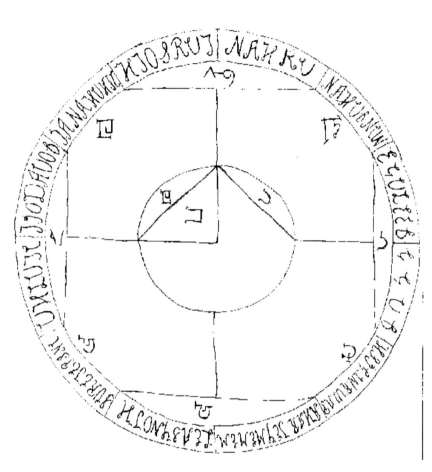

and it shall be made to the size of nine feet and it may be made for permenant of temporary use. At the north of the circle, three feet away, you will place the seal of the spirit which you wish to call. And the seal shall be written upon a circle of one foot of fine lamb skin or parchment. The ink used shall be that of a white pigeon's blood, which shall be killed with the knife and the blood collected in a new bowl. A pen shall be made from a feather of the bird. The creation of the circle and the seal shall be done eight hours prior to the rite of conjuration. If you would seek to evoke the Old Spirits then you must make the circle in the hour of Mercury, being eight hours before the conjuration. Once it has been created, the circle should not be entered until the ritual of evocation commences and the seal should be kept wrapped in white silk before the circle. And at the passing of every hour leading up to the ritual you shall banish and wandering spirits from the working area. First you shall make the Sign four times, saying each time: 'Iratisinger herikoramonus derogex Dalerinter'. Then you shall speak the following

Away! Away!

I command all wandering spirits to depart in

peace I command you, depart or face my wrath.

I am the he who howls the forgotten

names, I am he who shall bring forth the

spirit n.! Turn and face me, for I hold the

Sign!

Iratisinger

Herikoramons

Derogex

Daleringer

Now depart with
haste!

THE MAGAN TEXT

THE verses here following come from the secret text of some of the priests of a cult which is all that is left of the Old Faith that existed before Babylon was built, and it was originally in their tongue, but I have put it into the Golden Speech of my country so that you may understand it. I came upon this text in my early wanderings in the region of the Seven Fabled Cities of UR, which are no more, and it tells of the War between the Gods that took place in a time beyond the memory of man. And the horrors and ugliness that the Priest will encounter in his Rites are herein described, and their reasons, and their natures, and Essences. And the Number of the Lines is Sacred, and the Word are Sacred, and are most potent charms against the Evil Ones. And surely some Magicians of the country do write them on parchment or clay, or on pottery, or in the air, that they might be efficacious thereby, and that the Gods will remember the words of the Covenant.

I copied these words down in my tongue and kept them faithfully these many years, and my own copy will go with me to the place where I will go when my Spirit is torn from the body. But heed these words well, and remember! For remembering is the most important and most potent magick, being the Rememberance of Things Past and the Rememberance of Things to Come, which is the same Memory. And do not show this text to the uninitiated, for it hath caused madness, in men and in beasts.

The Text:

I

THE MAGAN TEXT

Hearken, and Remember!

In the Name of ANU, Remember!
In the Name of ENLIL, Remember!
In the Name of ENKI, Remember!
When on High the Heavens had not been named,
The Earth had not been named,
And Naught existed but the Seas of ABSU,
The Ancient One,
And MUMMU TIAMAT, the Ancient One
Who bore them all,
Their Waters as One Water.
At this time, before the ELDER GODS had been brought forth,
Uncalled by Name,
Their destinies unknown and undetermined,
Then it was that the Gods were formed within the Ancient Ones.
LLMU and LLAAMU were brought forth and called by Name,
And for Ages they grew in age and bearing.
ANSHAR and KISHAR were brought forth,
And brought forth ANU
Who begat NUDIMMUD, Our Master ENKI,
Who has no rival among the Gods. Remember!

The Elder Ones came together
They disturbed TIAMAT, the Ancient One, as they surged back and forth.
Yea, they troubled the belly of TIAMAT
By their Rebellion in the abode of Heaven.
ABSU could not lessen their clamour

TIAMAT was speechless at their ways.

Their doings were loathsome unto the Ancient Ones.

ABSU rose up to slay the Elder Gods by stealth.

With magick charm and spell ABSU fought,
But was slain by the sorcery of the Elder Gods.
And it was their first victory.
His body was lain in an empty Space
In a crevice of the heavens
Hid
He was lain,
But his blood cried out to the Abode of Heaven.

TIAMAT

Enraged
Filled with an Evil Motion Said
Let us make Monsters
That they may go out and do battle Against these Sons of
Iniquity

The murderous offspring who have destroyed A God.
HUBUR arose, She who fashioneth all things, And possessor of Magick
like unto Our Master.

She added matchless weapons to the arsenals of the Ancient Ones, She bore Monster-
Serpents
Sharp of tooth, long of fang,
She filled their bodies with venom for blood Roaring dragons she has
clothed with Terror

Has crowned them with Halos, making them as Gods, So that he who
beholds them shall perish
And, that, with their bodies reared up None might turn them
back.
She summoned the Viper, the Dragon, and the Winged Bull, The Great Lion, the
Mad-God, and the Scorpion-Man. Mighty rabid Demons, Feathered-Serpents, the
Horse-Man, Bearing weapons that spare no

Fearless in Battle,
Charmed with the spells of ancient sorcery,
. . . withal Eleven of this kind she brought forth With KINGU as
Leader of the Minions.

Remember!

ENKI

Our Master

Fearing defeat, summoned his Son

MARDUK
Summoned his Son
The Son of Magick
Told him the Secret Name
The Secret Number
The Secret Shape
Whereby he might do battle
With the Ancient Horde
And be victorious.

MARDUK KURIOS! Brightest Star among the Stars Strongest God
among the Gods Son of Magick and the Sword Child of Wisdom and
the Word Knower of the Secret Name Knower of the Secret Number
Knower of the Secret Shape

He armed himself with the Disc of Power In chariots of Fire he went forth
With a shouting Voice he called the Spell With a Blazing Flame he filled his
Body Dragons, Vipers, all fell down
Lions, Horse-Men, all were slain.
The Mighty creatures of HUBUR were slain
The Spells, the Charms, the Sorcery were broken. Naught but TIAMAT remained.
The Great Serpent, the Enormous Worm The Snake with iron teeth
The Snake with sharpened claw The Snake with Eyes of Death, She
lunged at MARDUK

With a roar With a curse She lunged.
MARDUK struck with the Disc of Power Blinded TIAMAT's Eyes of Death

The Monster heaved and raised its back Struck forth in all directions
Spitting ancient words of Power Screamed the ancient incantations
MARDUK struck again and blew An Evil Wind into her body

Which filled the raging, wicked Serpent MARDUK shot between her jaws

The Charmed arrow of ENKI's Magick

MARDUK struck again and severed
The head of TIAMAT from its body.

And all was silent.

Remember!

MARDUK Victor

Took the Tablets of Destiny Unbidden
Hung them around his neck. Acclaimed of the Elder Gods was he. First
among the Elder Ones was he.
He split the sundered TIAMAT in twain And fashioned the heavens and the
earth,

With a Gate to keep the Ancient Ones Without. With a Gate whose Key is hid
forever
Save to the Sons of MARDUK Save to the Followers of Our Master
ENKI
First in Magick among the Gods.

From the Blood of KINGU he fashioned Man. He constructed Watchtowers for
the Elder Gods Fixing their astral bodies as constellations

That they may watch the Gate of ABSU The Gate of TIAMAT they watch

The Gate of KINGU they oversee
The Gate whose Guardian is IAK SAKKAK they bind. All the Elder Powers resist
The Force of Ancient Artistry
The Magick Spell of the Oldest Ones
The Incantation of the Primal Power
The Mountain KUR, the Serpent God The Mountain MASHU, that of
Magick The Dead KUTULU, Dead but Dreaming TIAMAT, Dead but
Dreaming
ABSU, KINGU, Dead but Dreaming And shall their generation come again?

WE ARE THE LOST ONES From a Time before Time From a
Land beyond the Stars

From the Age when ANU walked the earth

In company of Bright Angels. We have survived
the first War Between the Powers of the Gods

And have seen the wrath of the Ancient Ones Dark Angels
Vent upon the Earth
WE ARE FROM A RACE BEYOND THE WANDERERS OF NIGHT. We have
survived the Age when ABSU ruled the Earth
And the Power destroyed out generations. We have survived
on tops of mountains And beneath the feet of mountains

And have spoken with the Scorpions In allegiance and
were betrayed.

And TIAMAT has promised us nevermore to attack With water and
with wind.
But the Gods are forgetful.
Beneath the Seas of NAR MATTARU
Beneath the Seas of the Earth, NAR MATTARU Beneath the
World lays sleeping
The God of Anger, Dead but Dreaming
The God of CUTHALU, Dead but Dreaming! The Lord of KUR,
calm but thunderous!

The One-Eyes Sword, cold but burning!

He who awakens Him calls the ancient Vengeance of
the Elder Ones

The Seven Glorious Gods
of the Seven Glorious Cities Upon himself and
upon the World And old vengeance . . .

Know that our years are the years of War

And our days are measured as battles
And every hour is a Life
Lost to the Outside
Those from Without
Have builded up charnel houses
To nourish the fiends of TIAMAT
And the Blood of the weakest here
Is libation unto TIAMAT
Queen of the Ghouls
Wreaker of Pain
And to invoke her
The Red Water of Life
Need be split on a stone
The stone struck with a sword

That hath slain eleven men

Sacrifices to HUBUR
So that the Strike ringeth out
And call TIAMAT from Her slumber
From her sleep in the Caverns
Of the Earth.

And none may dare entreat further

For to invoke Death is to utter
The final prayer.

II

Of the Generations of the Ancient Ones

UTUKK XUL

The account of the generations
Of the Ancient Ones here rendered
Of the generations of the Ancient Ones Here remembered.
Cold and Rain that erode all things They are the Evil Spirits
In the creation of ANU spawned Plague Gods
PAZUZU
And the Beloved Sons of ENG
The Offspring of NINNKIGAL
Rending in pieces on high Bringing destruction below They are Children of the
Underworld
Loudly roaring on high Gibbering loathsomely below

They are the bitter venom of the Gods. The great storms directed from
heaven Those are they
The Owl, Messenger of UGGI Lord of Death
Those they are
THEY ARE THE CHILDREN BORN OF EARTH

THAT IN THE CREATION

OF ANU WERE SPAWNED.

The highest walls The thickest walls
The strongest walls Like a flood they
pass From house to house They ravage

No door can shut them out No bolt can turn
them back
Through the door like snakes they slide Through the bolts
like winds they blow

Pulling the wife from the embrace of the husband Snatching the
child from the loins of man Banishing the man from his home, his
land THEY ARE THE BURNING PAIN
THAT PRESSETH ITSELF ON THE BACK OF MAN.

THEY ARE GHOULS

The spirit of the harlot that hath died in the streets The spirit of the
woman that hath died in childbirth
The spirit of the woman that hath dies, weeping with a babe at the breast The spirit of an
evil man
One that haunteth the streets Or one that
haunteth the bed. They are Seven!
Seven are they!
Those Seven were born in the Mountains of MASHU Called Magick
They dwell within the Caverns of the Earth Amid the desolate
places of the Earth they live Amid the places between
The Places
Unknown in heaven and in earth They are
arrayed in terror
Among the Elder Gods there is no knowledge of them They have no
name
Not in heaven Nor on earth

They ride over the Mountain of Sunset And on the
Mountain of Dawn they cry

Through the Caverns of the Earth they creep Amid the
desolate places of the Earth they lie Nowhere are they known
Not in heaven Nor in the Earth

Are they discovered

For their place is outside our place And between the angles of
the Earth They lie in wait
Crouching for the Sacrifice
THEY ARE THEY CHILDREN OF THE UNDERWORLD.

Falling like rain from the sky Issuing like mist from the
earth Doors do not stop them

Bolts do not stop them
They glide in at the doors like serpents They enter by the windows like
the wind IDPA they are, entering by the head NAMTAR they are,
entering by the heart UTUK they are, entering by the brow ALAL they
are, entering by the chest GIGIM they are, seizing the bowels TELAL
they are, grasping the hand

URUKU they are, giant Larvae, feeding on the Blood They are Seven!
Seven are They!
They seize all the towers From UR to NIPPUR Yet UR
knows them not

Yet NIPPUR does not know them They have brought down the
mighty Of all the mighty Cities of man

Yet man knows them not
Yes the Cities do not know them
They have struck down the forests of the East And have flooded the
Lands of the West
Yet the East knows them not
Yet the West does not know them They are a hand grasping at
the neck Yet the neck does not know them And man knows them
not.
Their words are Unwrit Their numbers are Unknown
Their shapes are all Shapes Their habitations
The desolate places where their Rites are performed Their habitations
The haunts of man where a sacrifice has been offered Their habitations
The lands here

And cities here

And the lands between the lands The cities between the cities

In spaces no man has ever walked In KURNUDE
The country from whence no traveller returns At EKURBAD
In the altar of the Temple of the Dead And at GI UMUNA
At their Mother's breast
At the Foundations of CHAOS

In the ARALIYA of MUMMU-TIAMAT And at the Gates
Of IAK SAKKAK!

SPIRIT OF THE AIR, REMEMBER!

SPIRIT OF THE EARTH, REMEMBER!

III

Of the Forgotten Generations of Man

And was not Man created from the blood of KINGU Commander of the hordes of
the Ancient Ones? Does not man possess in his spirit

The sees of rebellion against the Elder Gods? And the blood of Man is the Blood of
Vengeance And the blood of Man is the Spirit of Vengeance

And the Power of Man is the Power of the Ancient Ones And this is the Covenant
For, lo! The Elder Gods possess the Sign
By which the Powers of the Ancient Ones are turned back But Man possesses the Sign
And the Number
And the Shape
To summon the Blood of his Parents. And this is the Covenant.
Created by the Elder Gods
From the Blood of the Ancient Ones Man is the Key by which
The Gate if IAK SAKKAK may be flung wide By which the Ancient Ones
Seek their Vengeance Upon the face of the Earth

Against the Offspring of MARDUK. For what is new

Came from that which is old And what is old
Shall replace that which is new And once again the Ancient Ones

Shall rule upon the face of the Earth! And this is too the Covenant!

IV

Of the Sleep of ISHTAR

Yet ISHTAR Queen of Heaven

Bright Light of Nights
Mistress of the Gods
Set her mind in that direction From Above she set her mind, To Below she
set her mind From the Heavens she set forth To the Abyss
Out of the Gates of the Living To enter the Gates of Death Out of the Lands
we know Into the Lands we know not To the Land of No Return

To the Land of Queen ERESHKIGAL ISHTAR, Queen of Heavens, she set her mind
ISHTAR, Daughter of SIN, she set forth
To the Black Earth, the Land of CUTHA She set forth
To the House of No Return she set her foot Upon the Road whence None Return
She set her foot
To the Cave, forever unlit
Where bowls of clay are heaped upon the alter Where bowls of dust are the food
Of residents clothed only in wings To ABSU ISHTAR set forth.

Where sleeps the dread CUTHALU

ISHTAR set forth.

The Watcher

Stood fast.
The Watcher
NINNGHIZHIDDA
Stood fast.
And ISHTAR spoke unto him

NINNGHIZHIDDA! Serpent of the Deep!
NINNGHIZHIDDA! Horned Serpent of the Deep!
NINNGHIZHIDDA! Plumed Serpent of the Deep! Open!

Open the Door that I may enter!
NINNGHIZHIDDA, Spirit of the Deep, Watcher of the Gate, Remember!
In the Name of our Father before the Flight, ENKI, Lord and Master of Magicians Open
the Door that I may enter!
Open
Lest I attack the Door Lest I break
apart its bars Lest I attack the
Barrier

Lest I take its walls by force Open
the Door
Open Wide the Gate
Lest I cause the Dead to rise! I will
raise up the Dead!

I will cause the Dead to rise and devour the living! Open
the Door
Lest I cause the Dead to outnumber the Living! NINNGHIZHIDDA, Spirit of
the Deep, Watcher of the Gate, Open!

NINNGHIZHIDDA

The Great Serpent
Coiled back on itself
And answered
ISHTAR
Lady
Queen among the Gods
I go before my Mistress
ERESHKIGAL
Before the Queen of Death
I will announce Thee.

And NINNGHIZHIDDA

Horned Serpent

Approached the Lady ERESHKIGAL

And said:
Behold, ISHTAR, Thy Sister
Queen among the Gods
Stands before the Gate!
Daughter of SIN, Mistress of ENKI
She waits.

And ERESHKIGAL was pale with fear.

The Dark Waters stirred.

Go, Watcher of the Gate.

Go, NINNGHIZHIDDA, Watcher of the Gate, Open the Door to ISHTAR
And treat Her as it is written In the Ancient Covenant.

And NINNGHIZHIDDA loosed the bolt from the hatch And Darkness fell upon ISHTAR

The Dark Waters rose and carried the Goddess of Light To the Realms of the Night.
And the Serpent spoke: Enter
Queen of Heaven of the Great Above That KUR may rejoice
That CUTHA may give praise That KUTU may smile. Enter
That KUTULU may be pleased at Thy presence

And ISHTAR entered.

And there are Seven gates and Seven Decrees.

At the First Gate

NINGHIZHIDDA removed the Crown The Great Crown of Her head he took
away And ISHTAR asked

Why, Serpent, has thou removed my First Jewel? And the Serpent answered
Thus is, the Covenant of Old, set down before Time, The Rules of the Lady of KUTU.
Enter the First Gate.

And the Second Gate

NINNGHIZHIDDA removed the Wand

The Wand of Lapis Lazuli he took away
And ISHTAR asked
Why, NETI, has thou removed my Second Jewel?
And NETI answered
Thus it is, the Covenant of Old, set down before Time
The Decrees of the Lady of KUTU.
Enter the Second Gate.

At the Third Gate

NINNGHIZHIDDA removed the Jewels

The Jewels around her neck he took away
And ISHTAR asked
Why, Gatekeeper, has thou removed my Third Jewel?
And the Gatekeeper answered
Thus it is, the Covenant of Old, set down before Time,
The Decrees of the Lady of KUTU
Enter the Third Gate.

At the Fourth Gate

NINGHIZHIDDA removed the Jewels The Jewels
on her breast he took away And ISHTAR asked

Why, Guardian of the Outer, has thou removed my Fourth Jewel? And the
Guardian answered
Thus it is, the Covenant of Old, set down before Time, The Rules
of the Lady of KUTU.
Enter the Fourth Gate.

At the Fifth Gate

NINNGHIZHIDDA removed the Jewels

The Belt of Jewels around her hips he took away And
ISHTAR asked
Why, Watcher of the Forbidden Entrance, hast thou removed my Fifth Jewel? And the
Watcher answered
Thus it is, the Covenant of Old, set down before Time, The Rules
of the Lady of KUTUK.
Enter the Fifth Gate. At the Sixth
Gate

NINNGHIZHIDDA removed the Jewels The Jewels
around her wrists
And the Jewels around her ankles he took away.

And ISHTAR asked

Why, NINNKIGAL, hast thou removed my Sixth Jewel?
And NINKIGAL answered
Thus it is, the ancient Covenant, set down before Time,
The Decrees of Lady of KUTU.
Enter the Sixth Gate.

At the Seventh Gate

NINNGHIZHIDDA removed the Jewels

The Jewelled Robes of ISHTAR he took away. ISHTAR,
without protection, without safety, ISHTAR, without talisman
or amulet, asked

Why, Messenger of the Ancient Ones, hast thou removed my Seventh Jewel? And the
Messenger of the Ancient Ones replied
Thus it is, the Covenant of Old, set down before Time, The Rules
of the Lady of KUTU.
Enter the Seventh Gate and behold the Nether World.

ISHTAR had descended to the Land of KUR

To the Depths of CUTHA she went down.
Having lost her Seven Talisman of the Upper Worlds
Having lost her Seven Powers of the Land of the Living
Without Food of Life or Water of Life
She appeared before ERESHKIGAL, Mistress of Death.
ERESHKIGAL screamed at Her presence.

ISHTAR raised up Her arm.

ERESHKIGAL summoned NAMMTAR
The Magician NAMMTAR
Saying these words she spoke to him
Go! Imprison her!
Bind her in Darkness!
Chain her in the Sea below the Seas!
Release against her the Seven ANNUNNAKI!
Release against her the Sixty Demons!
Against her eyes, the demons of the eyes!
Against her sides, the demons of the sides!
Against her heart, the demons of the heart!
Against her feet, the demons of the feet!
Against her head, the demons of the head!
Against her entire body, the demons the KUR!

And the demons tore at her, from every side.

And the ANNUNAKI, Dread Judges Seven Lords of the
Underworld Drew Around Her

Faceless Gods of ABSU They stared
Fixed her with the Eye of Death Withe the Glance of Death
They killed her
And hung her like a corpse from a stake
The sixty demons tearing her limbs from her sides Her eyes from her head

Her ears from her skull.

ERESHKIGAL rejoiced. Blind AZAG-THOTH rejoiced
IAK SAKKAK rejoiced ISHNIGGARRAB rejoiced
KUTULU rejoiced

The MASKIM gave praise to the Queen of Death
The GIGIM gave praise to ERESHKIGAL, Queen of Death.

And the Elder Ones were rent with fear.

Our Father ENKI

Lord of Magick
Receiving   word   by   NINSHUBUR   ISHTAR's   servant
NINSHUBUR He hears of ISHTAR's Sleep

In the House of Death
He hears how GANZIR has been Opened
How the Face of Abyss Opened wide its mouth

And swallowed the Queen of Heaven Queen of the Rising of the Sun.

And ENKI summoned forth clay And ENKI summoned forth wind
And from the clay and from the wind ANKI fashioned two
Elementals

He fashioned the KURGARRU, spirit of the Earth, He fashioned the
KALATURRU, spirit of the Seas, To the KURGARRU he gave the Food of Life

To the KALATURRU he gave the Water of Life And to these images he
spoke aloud
Arise, KALATURRU, Spirit of the Seas

Arise, and set thy feet to that Gate GANZIR To the Gate of the
Underworld

The Land of No Return Set thine eyes
The Seven Gates shall open for thee No spell shall keep thee out
For my Number is upon you. Take the bag of the Food of Life
Take the bag of the Water of Life

And ERESHKIGAL shall not raise her arm against you ERESHKIGAL SHALL HAVE NO
POWER OVER YOU.

Find the corpse of INANNA

Find the corpse of ISHTAR our Queen And sprinkle the Food of Life,
Sixty Times And sprinkle the Water of Life, Sixty Times
Sixty Times the Food of Life and the Water of Life Sprinkle upon her body
And truly ISHTAR will rise.

With giant wings

And scales like serpents
The two elementals flew to that Gate
Invisible
NINNGHIZHIDDA saw them not
Invisible
They passes the Seven Watchers
With haste they entered the Palace of Death
And they beheld several terrible sights.

The demons of all the Abyss lay there Dead but Dreaming, they clung to
the walls Of the House of Death

Faceless and terrible
The ANNUNAKI stared out
Blind and Mad AZAG-THOTH reared up The Eye on the Throne
opened
The Dark Waters stirred
The Gates of Lapis Lazuli glistened In the darkness
Unseen Monsters
Spawned at the Dawn of Ages
Spawned in the Battle of MARDUK and TIAMAT Spawned in HUBUR
With the Sign of HUBUR

Lead by KINGU . . .

With haste they fled Through the Palace of Death

Stopping only at the corpse of ISHTAR

The Beautiful Queen

Mistress of the Gods
Lady of all the Harlots of UR Bright Shining One of the Heavens Beloved of ENKI
Lay hung and bleeding
From a thousand fatal wounds.

ERESHKIGAL

Sensing their presence
Cried out.

KUGAARU Armed with Fire

Looked upon the Queen of Corpses with the Ray of Fire

KALATURRU Armed with Flame

Looked upon the Queen of the Graves With the Rays of Flame.

And ERESHKIGAL

Mighty in CUTHA
Turned her face

Upon the corpse of INANNA

Sixty times they sprinkled
The Water of Life of ENKI
Upon the corpse of ISHTAR
Sixty times they sprinkled
The Food of Life of ENKI

Upon the corpse Hung from a stake

They directed the Spirit of Life INANNA AROSE.

The Dark Waters trembled and roiled.

AZAG-THOTH screamed upon his throne CUTHALU lurched forth from his sleep
ISHNIGARRAB fled the Palace of Death IAK SAKKAK trembled in fear and hate
The ANNUNNAKI fled their thrones The Eye upon the Throne took flight

ERESHKIGAL roared and summoned NAMMTAR The Magician NAMMRAR she called
But not for pursuit But for protection.

INANNA ascended from the Underworld.

With the winged elementals she fled the Gates Of GANZIR and NETI she fled

And verily
The Dead fled ahead of her.

When through the First Gate they fled

ISHTAR took back her jewelled robes.

When through the Second Gate they fled ISHTAR took back her jewelled
bracelets.

When through the Third Gate they fled

ISHTAR took back her jewelled belt.

When through the Fourth Gate they fled ISHTAR took back her jewelled necklace.

When through the Fifth Gate they fled

ISHTAR took back her Belt of Jewels.

When through the Sixth Gate they fled

ISHTAR took back her Wand of Lapis

When through the Seventh Gate they fled ISHTAR took back her jewelled crown.

And the Demons rose

And the Spirits of the Dead
And went with her out of the Gates Looking neither right nor left
Walking in front and behind
They went with ISHTAR from the Gate of GANZIR Out of the Netherworld they
accompanied her

And ERESHKIGAL

Scorned Queen of the Abyss Wherein All Are Drowned Pronounced a Curse Solemn and
Powerful
Against the Queen of the Rising of the Sun And
NAMMTAR gave it form.

When the Lover of ISHTAR

Beloved of the Queen of Heaven
Goes down before me
Goes through the Gate of GANZIR
To the House of Death
When with him the wailing people come
The weeping woman and the wailing man

When DUMUZI is slain and buried
MAY THE DEAD RISE AND SMELL THE INCENSE!

V

Stoop not down, therefore,

Unto the Darkly Shining World
Where the ABSU lies in Dark Waters
And CUTHALU sleeps and dreams

Stoop not down, therefore,

For an Abyss lies beneath the World
Reached by a descending Ladder
That hath Seven Steps
Reached by a descending Pathway
That hath Seven Gates
And therein is established
The Throne
Of an Evil and Fatal Force.
For from the Cavities of the World
Leaps forth the Evil Demon
The Evil God
The Evil Genius
The Evil Ensnarer
The Evil Phantom
The Evil Devil
The Evil Larvae

Showing no true Signs

Unto mortal Man.
AND THE DEAD WILL RISE AND SMELL THE INCENSE!

ENUMA ELISH
THE EPIC OF CREATION

THE FIRST TABLET

When in the height heaven was not named,
And the earth beneath did not yet bear a name,
And the primeval Apsu, who begat them,
And chaos, Tiamut, the mother of them both
Their waters were mingled together,
And no field was formed, no marsh was to be seen;
When of the gods none had been called into being,
And none bore a name, and no destinies were ordained;
Then were created the gods in the midst of heaven,
Lahmu and Lahamu were called into being...
Ages increased,...
Then Ansar and Kisar were created, and over them....
Long were the days, then there came forth.....
Anu, their son,...
Ansar and Anu...
And the god Anu...
Nudimmud, whom his fathers, his begetters.....
Abounding in all wisdom,...'
He was exceeding strong...
He had no rival -
Thus were established and were... the great gods.
But Tiamat and Apsu were still in confusion...
They were troubled and...
In disorder...
Apru was not diminished in might...
And Tiamat roared...
She smote, and their deeds...
Their way was evil...
Then Apsu, the begetter of the great gods,
Cried unto Mummu, his minister, and said unto him:
"O Mummu, thou minister that rejoicest my spirit,
Come, unto Tiamut let us go!
So they went and before Tiamat they lay down,
They consulted on a plan with regard to the gods, their sons.
Apsu opened his mouth and spake,
And unto Tiamut, the glistening one, he addressed the word:
...their way...
By day I can not rest, by night I can not lie down in peace.
But I will destroy their way, I will...
Let there be lamentation, and let us lie down again in peace."

When Tiamat heard these words,
She raged and cried aloud...
She... grievously...,
She uttered a curse, and unto Apsu she spake:
"What then shall we do?
Let their way be made difficult, and let us lie down again in peace."
Mummu answered, and gave counsel unto Apsu,
...and hostile to the gods was the counsel Mummu gave:
Come, their way is strong, but thou shalt destroy it;
Then by day shalt thou have rest, by night shalt thou lie down in peace."
Apsu harkened unto him and his countenance grew bright,
Since he (Mummu) planned evil against the gods his sons.
... he was afraid...,
His knees became weak; they gave way beneath him,
Because of the evil which their first-born had planned.
... their... they altered.
... they...,
Lamentation they sat in sorrow
....
Then Ea, who knoweth all that is, went up and he beheld their muttering.

[about 30 illegible lines]

... he spake:
... thy... he hath conquered and
... he weepeth and sitteth in tribulation.
... of fear,
... we shall not lie down in peace.
... Apsu is laid waste,
... and Mummu, who were taken captive, in...
... thou didst...
... let us lie down in peace.
... they will smite....
... let us lie down in peace.
... thou shalt take vengeance for them,
... unto the tempest shalt thou...!"
And Tiamat harkened unto the word of the bright god, and said:
... shalt thou entrust! let us wage war!"
... the gods in the midst of...
... for the gods did she create.
They banded themselves together and at the side of Tiamat they advanced;
They were furious; they devised mischief without resting night and day.
They prepared for battle, fuming and raging;
They joined their forces and made war,
Ummu-Hubur [Tiamat] who formed all things,
Made in addition weapons invincible; she spawned monster-serpents,

Sharp of tooth, and merciless of fang;
With poison, instead of blood, she filled their bodies.
Fierce monster-vipers she clothed with terror,
With splendor she decked them, she made them of lofty stature.
Whoever beheld them, terror overcame him,
Their bodies reared up and none could withstand their attack.
She set up vipers and dragons, and the monster Lahamu,
And hurricanes, and raging hounds, and scorpion-men,
And mighty tempests, and fish-men, and rams;
They bore cruel weapons, without fear of the fight.
Her commands were mighty, none could resist them;
After this fashion, huge of stature, she made eleven [kinds of] monsters.
Among the gods who were her sons, inasmuch as he had given her support,
She exalted Kingu; in their midst she raised him to power.
To march before the forces, to lead the host,
To give the battle-signal, to advance to the attack,
To direct the battle, to control the fight,
Unto him she entrusted; in costly raiment she made him sit, saying:
I have uttered thy spell, in the assembly of the gods I have raised thee to power.
The dominion over all the gods have I entrusted unto him.
Be thou exalted, thou my chosen spouse,
May they magnify thy name over all of them the Anunnaki."
She gave him the Tablets of Destiny, on his breast she laid them, saying:
Thy command shall not be without avail, and the word of thy mouth shall be established."
Now Kingu, thus exalted, having received the power of Anu,
Decreed the fate among the gods his sons, saying:
"Let the opening of your mouth quench the Fire-god;
Whoso is exalted in the battle, let him display his might!"

THE SECOND TABLET

Tiamat made weighty her handiwork,
Evil she wrought against the gods her children.
To avenge Apsu, Tiamat planned evil,
But how she had collected her forces, the god unto Ea divulged.
Ea harkened to this thing, and
He was grievously afflicted and he sat in sorrow.
The days went by, and his anger was appeased,
And to the place of Ansar his father he took his way.
He went and, standing before Ansar, the father who begat him,
All that Tiamat had plotted he repeated unto him,
Saying, "Tiamat our mother hath conceived a hatred for us,
With all her force she rageth, full of wrath.
All the gods have turned to her,
With those, whom ye created, they go at her side.
They are banded together and at the side of Tiamat they advance;

They are furious, they devise mischief without resting night and day.
They prepare for battle, fuming and raging;
They have joined their forces and are making war.
Ummu-Hubur, who formed all things,
Hath made in addition weapons invincible; she hath spawned monster-serpents,
Sharp of tooth, and merciless of fang.
With poison, instead of blood, she hath filled their bodies.
Fierce monster-vipers she hath clothed with terror,
With splendor she hath decked them; she hath made them of lofty stature.
Whoever beholdeth them is overcome by terror,
Their bodies rear up and none can withstand their attack.
She hath set up vipers, and dragons, and the monster Lahamu,
And hurricanes and raging hounds, and scorpion-men,
And mighty tempests, and fish-men and rams;
They bear cruel weapons, without fear of the fight.
Her commands are mighty; none can resist them;
After this fashion, huge of stature, hath she made eleven monsters.
Among the gods who are her sons, inasmuch as he hath given her support,
She hath exalted Kingu; in their midst she hath raised him to power.
To march before the forces, to lead the host,
To give the battle-signal, to advance to the attack.
To direct the battle, to control the fight,
Unto him hath she entrusted; in costly raiment she hath made him sit, saving:.
I have uttered thy spell; in the assembly of the gods I have raised thee to power,
The dominion over all the gods have I entrusted unto thee.
Be thou exalted, thou my chosen spouse,
May they magnify thy name over all of them
She hath given him the Tablets of Destiny, on his breast she laid them, saying:
'Thy command shall not be without avail, and the word of thy mouth shall be established.'
Now Kingu, thus exalted, having received the power of Anu,
Decreed the fate for the gods, her sons, saying:
'Let the opening of your mouth quench the Fire-god;
Whoso is exalted in the battle, let him display his might!'"
When Ansar heard how Tiamat was mightily in revolt,
he bit his lips, his mind was not at peace,
..., he made a bitter lamentation:
... battle,
... thou...
Mummu and Apsu thou hast smitten
But Tiamat hath exalted Kingu, and where is one who can oppose her?
... deliberation
... the ... of the gods, -Nudimmud.

[A gap of about a dozen lines occurs here.]

Ansar unto his son addressed the word:

"... my mighty hero,
Whose strength is great and whose onslaught can not be withstood,
Go and stand before Tiamat,
That her spirit may be appeased, that her heart may be merciful.
But if she will not harken unto thy word,
Our word shalt thou speak unto her, that she may be pacified."
He heard the word of his father Ansar
And he directed his path to her, toward her he took the way.
Ann drew nigh, he beheld the muttering of Tiamat,
But he could not withstand her, and he turned back.
... Ansar
... he spake unto him:

[A gap of over twenty lines occurs here.]

an avenger...
... valiant
... in the place of his decision
... he spake unto him:
... thy father
" Thou art my son, who maketh merciful his heart.
... to the battle shalt thou draw nigh,
he that shall behold thee shall have peace."
And the lord rejoiced at the word of his father,
And he drew nigh and stood before Ansar.
Ansar beheld him and his heart was filled with joy,
He kissed him on the lips and his fear departed from him.
"O my father, let not the word of thy lips be overcome,
Let me go, that I may accomplish all that is in thy heart.
O Ansar, let not the word of thy lips be overcome,
Let me go, that I may accomplish all that is in thy heart."
What man is it, who hath brought thee forth to battle?
... Tiamat, who is a woman, is armed and attacketh thee.
... rejoice and be glad;
The neck of Tiamat shalt thou swiftly trample under foot.
... rejoice and be glad;
The neck of Tiamat shalt thou swiftly trample under foot.
0 my son, who knoweth all wisdom,
Pacify Tiamat with thy pure incantation.
Speedily set out upon thy way,
For thy blood shall not be poured out; thou shalt return again."
The lord rejoiced at the word of his father,
His heart exulted, and unto his father he spake:
"O Lord of the gods, Destiny of the great gods,
If I, your avenger,
Conquer Tiamat and give you life,

Appoint an assembly, make my fate preeminent and proclaim it.
In Upsukkinaku seat yourself joyfully together,
With my word in place of you will I decree fate.
May whatsoever I do remain unaltered,
May the word of my lips never be chanced nor made of no avail."

THE THIRD TABLET

Ansar opened his mouth, and
Unto Gaga, his minister, spake the word.
"O Gaga, thou minister that rejoicest my spirit,
Unto Lahmu and Lahamu will I send thee.
... thou canst attain,
... thou shalt cause to be brought before thee.
... let the gods, all of them,
Make ready for a feast, at a banquet let them sit,
Let them eat bread, let them mix wine,
That for Marduk, their avenger they may decree the fate.
Go, Gaga, stand before them,
And all that I tell thee, repeat unto them, and say:
'Ansar, vour son, hath sent me,
The purpose of his heart he hath made known unto me.
The purpose of his heart he hath made known unto me.
He saith that Tiamat our mother hath conceived a hatred for us,
With all her force she rageth, full of wrath.
All the gods have turned to her,
With those, whom ye created, they go at her side.
They are banded together, and at the side of Tiamat they advance;
They are furious, they devise mischief without resting night and day.
They prepare for battle, fuming and raging;
They have joined their forces and are making war.
Ummu-Hubur, who formed all things,
Hath made in addition weapons invincible; she hath spawned monster-serpents,
Sharp of tooth and merciless of fang.
With poison, instead of blood, she hath filled their bodies.
Fierce monster-vipers she hath clothed with terror,
With splendor she hath decked them; she hath made them of lofty stature.
Whoever beboldeth them, terror overcometh him,
Their bodies rear up and none can withstand their attack.
She hath set up vipers, and dragons, and the monster Lahamu,
And hurricanes, and raging bounds, and scorpion-men,
And mighty tempests, and fish-men, and rams;
They bear merciless weapons, without fear of the fight.
Her commands are miahty; none can. resist them;
After this fashion, huge of stature, hath she made eleven monsters.

Among the gods who are her sons, inasmuch as he hath given her support,
She hath exalted Kingu; in their midst she hath raised him to power.
To march before the forces, to lead the host,
To give the battle-signal, to advance to the attack,
To direct the battle, to control the fight,
Unto him hath she entrusted; in costly raiment she hath made him sit, saying:
I have uttered thy spell; in the assembly of the gods
I have raised thee to power,
The dominion over all the gods have I entrusted unto thee.
Be thou exalted, thou my chosen spouse,
May they magnify thy name over all of them ... the Anunnaki."
She hath given him the Tablets of Destiny, on his breast she laid them, saying:
Thy command shall not be without avail, and the word of thy mouth shall be established."
Now Kingu, thus exalted, having received the power of Anu,
Decreed the fate for the gods, her sons, saying:
Let the opening of your mouth quench the Fire-god;
Whoso is exalted in the battle, let him display his might!"
I sent Anu, but he could not withstand her;
Nudimmud was afraid and turned back.
But Marduk hath set out, the director of the gods, your son;
To set out against Tiamat his heart hath prompted him.
He opened his mouth and spake unto me, saying: "If I, your avenger,
Conquer Tiamat and give you life,
Appoint an assembly, make my fate preeminent and proclaim it.
In Upsukkinaku seat yourself joyfully together;
With my word in place of you will I decree fate.
May whatsoever I do remain unaltered,
May the word of my lips never be changed nor made of no avail.'"
Hasten, therefore, and swiftly decree for him the fate which you bestow,
That he may go and fight your strong enemy.
Gaga went, he took his way and
Humbly before Lahmu and Lahamu, the gods, his fathers,
He made obeisance, and he kissed the ground at their feet.
He humbled himself; then he stood up and spake unto them saying:
"Ansar, your son, hath sent me,
The purpose of his heart he hath made known unto me.
He saith that Tiamat our mother hath conceived a hatred for us,
With all her force she rageth, full of wrath.
All the gods have turned to her,
With those, whom ye created, they go at her side.
They are banded together and at the side of Tiamat they advance;
They are furious, they devise mischief without resting night and day.
They prepare for battle, fuming and raging;
They have joined their forces and are making war.
Ummu-Hubur, who formed all things,
Hath made in addition weapons invincible; she hath spawned monster-serpents,

Sharp of tooth and merciless of fang.
With poison, instead of blood, she hath filled their bodies.
Fierce monster-vipers she hath clothed with terror,
With splendor she hath decked them, she hath made them of lofty stature.
Whoever beboldeth them, terror overcometh him,
Their bodies rear up and none can withstand their attack.
She hath set up vipers, and dragons, and the monster Lahamu,
And hurricanes, and raging hounds, and scorpion-men,
And mighty tempests, and fish-men, and rams;
They bear merciless weapons, without fear of the fight.
Her commands are mighty; none can resist them;
After this fashion, huge of stature, hath she made eleven monsters.
Among the gods who are her sons, inasmuch as he hath given her support,
She hath exalted Kingu; in their midst she hath raised him to power.
To march before the forces, to lead the host,
To give the battle-signal, to advance to the attack, To direct the battle, to control the fight,
Unto him hath she entrusted; in costly raiment she hath made him sit, saving:
I have uttered thy spell; in the assembly of the gods I have raised thee to power,
The dominion over all the gods have I entrusted unto thee.
Be thou exalted, thou my chosen spouse,
May they magnify thy name over all of them...the Anunnaki.
She hath given him the Tablets of Destiny on his breast she laid them, saving:
Thy command shall not be without avail, and the word of thy mouth shall be established.'
Now Kingu, thus exalted, having received the power of Anu,
Decreed the fate for the gods, her sons, saying:
'Let the opening of your mouth quench the Fire-god;
Whoso is exalted in the battle, let him display his might!'
I sent Anu, but he could not withstand her;
Nudimmud was afraid and turned back.
But Marduk hath set out, the director of the gods, your son;
To set out against Tiamat his heart hath prompted him.
He opened his mouth and spake unto me, saying:
'If I, your avenger,
Conquer Tiamat and give you life,
Appoint an assembly, make my fate preeminent and proclaim it.
In Upsukkinaku seat yourselves joyfully together;
With my word in place of you will I decree fate.
May, whatsoever I do remain unaltered,
May the word of my lips never be changed nor made of no avail.'
Hasten, therefore, and swiftly decree for him the fate which you bestow,
That he may go and fight your strong enemy!
Lahmu and Lahamu heard and cried aloud
All of the Igigi [The elder gods] wailed bitterly, saying:
What has been altered so that they should
We do not understand the deed of Tiamat!
Then did they collect and go,

The great gods, all of them, who decree fate.
They entered in before Ansar, they filled...
They kissed one another, in the assembly...;
They made ready for the feast, at the banquet they sat;
They ate bread, they mixed sesame-wine.
The sweet drink, the mead, confused their...
They were drunk with drinking, their bodies were filled.
They were wholly at ease, their spirit was exalted;
Then for Marduk, their avenger, did they decree the fate.

THE FOURTH TABLET

They prepared for him a lordly chamber,
Before his fathers as prince he took his place.
"Thou art chiefest among the great gods,
Thy fate is unequaled, thy word is Anu!
O Marduk, thou art chiefest among the great gods,
Thy fate is unequaled, thy word is Anu!
Henceforth not without avail shall be thy command,
In thy power shall it be to exalt and to abase.
Established shall be the word of thy mouth, irresistible shall be thy command,
None among the gods shall transgress thy boundary.
Abundance, the desire of the shrines of the gods,
Shall be established in thy sanctuary, even though they lack offerings.
O Marduk, thou art our avenger!
We give thee sovereignty over the whole world.
Sit thou down in might; be exalted in thy command.
Thy weapon shall never lose its power; it shall crush thy foe.
O Lord, spare the life of him that putteth his trust in thee,
But as for the god who began the rebellion, pour out his life."
Then set they in their midst a garment,
And unto Marduk,- their first-born they spake:
"May thy fate, O lord, be supreme among the gods,
To destroy and to create; speak thou the word, and thy command shall be fulfilled.
Command now and let the garment vanish;
And speak the word again and let the garment reappear!
Then he spake with his mouth, and the garment vanished;
Again he commanded it, and. the garment reappeared.
When the gods, his fathers, beheld the fulfillment of his word,
They rejoiced, and they did homage unto him, saying, " Marduk is king!"
They bestowed upon him the scepter, and the throne, and the ring,
They give him an invincible weapony which overwhelmeth the foe.
Go, and cut off the life of Tiamat,
And let the wind carry her blood into secret places."
After the gods his fathers had decreed for the lord his fate,
They caused him to set out on a path of prosperity and success.

He made ready the bow, he chose his weapon,
He slung a spear upon him and fastened it...
He raised the club, in his right hand he grasped it,
The bow and the quiver he hung at his side.
He set the lightning in front of him,
With burning flame he filled his body.
He made a net to enclose the inward parts of Tiamat,
The four winds he stationed so that nothing of her might escape;
The South wind and the North wind and the East wind and the West wind
He brought near to the net, the gift of his father Anu.
He created the evil wind, and the tempest, and the hurricane,
And the fourfold wind, and the sevenfold wind, and the whirlwind, and the wind which
had no equal;
He sent forth the winds which he had created, the seven of them;
To disturb the inward parts of Tiamat, they followed after him.
Then the lord raised the thunderbolt, his mighty weapon,
He mounted the chariot, the storm unequaled for terror,
He harnessed and yoked unto it four horses,
Destructive, ferocious, overwhelming, and swift of pace;
... were their teeth, they were flecked with foam;
They were skilled in... , they had been trained to trample underfoot.
... . mighty in battle,
Left and right....
His garment was... , he was clothed with terror,
With overpowering brightness his head was crowned.
Then he set out, he took his way,
And toward the raging Tiamat he set his face.
On his lips he held ...,
... he grasped in his hand.
Then they beheld him, the gods beheld him,
The gods his fathers beheld him, the gods beheld him.
And the lord drew nigh, he gazed upon the inward parts of Tiamat,
He perceived the muttering of Kingu, her spouse.
As Marduk gazed, Kingu was troubled in his gait,
His will was destroyed and his motions ceased.
And the gods, his helpers, who marched by his side,
Beheld their leader's..., and their sight was troubled.
But Tiamat... , she turned not her neck,
With lips that failed not she uttered rebellious words:
"... thy coming as lord of the gods,
From their places have they gathered, in thy place are they! "
Then the lord raised the thunderbolt, his mighty weapon,
And against Tiamat, who was raging, thus he sent the word:
Thou art become great, thou hast exalted thyself on high,
And thy heart hath prompted thee to call to battle.
... their fathers...,

... their... thou hatest...
Thou hast exalted Kingu to be thy spouse,
Thou hast... him, that, even as Anu, he should issue deerees.
thou hast followed after evil,
And against the gods my fathers thou hast contrived thy wicked plan.
Let then thy host be equipped, let thy weapons be girded on!
Stand! I and thou, let us join battle!
When Tiamat heard these words,
She was like one posessed, .she lost her reason.
Tiamat uttered wild, piercing cries,
She trembled and shook to her very foundations.
She recited an incantation, she pronounced her spell,
And the gods of the battle cried out for their weapons.
Then advanced Tiamat and Marduk, the counselor of the gods;
To the fight they came on, to the battle they drew nigh.
The lord spread out his net and caught her,
And the evil wind that was behind him he let loose in her face.
As Tiamat opened her mouth to its full extent,
He drove in the evil wind, while as yet she had not shut her lips.
The terrible winds filled her belly,
And her courage was taken from her, and her mouth she opened wide.
He seized the spear and burst her belly,
He severed her inward parts, he pierced her heart.
He overcame her and cut off her life;
He cast down her body and stood upon it.
When he had slain Tiamat, the leader,
Her might was broken, her host was scattered.
And the gods her helpers, who marched by her side,
Trembled, and were afraid, and turned back.
They took to flight to save their lives;
But they were surrounded, so that they could not escape.
He took them captive, he broke their weapons;
In the net they were caught and in the snare they sat down.
The ... of the world they filled with cries of grief.
They received punishment from him, they were held in bondage.
And on the eleven creatures which she had filled with the power of striking terror,
Upon the troop of devils, who marched at her...,
He brought affliction, their strength he...;
Them and their opposition he trampled under his feet.
Moreover, Kingu, who had been exalted over them,
He conquered, and with the god Dug-ga he counted him.
He took from him the Tablets of Destiny that were not rightly his,
He sealed them with a seal and in his own breast he laid them.
Now after the hero Marduk had conquered and cast down his enemies,
And had made the arrogant foe even like
And had fully established Ansar's triumph over the enemy

And had attained the purpose of Nudimmud,
Over the captive gods he strengthened his durance,
And unto Tiamat, whom he had conquered, he returned.
And the lord stood upon Tiamat's hinder parts,
And with his merciless club he smashed her skull.
He cut through the channels of her blood,
And he made the North wind bear it away into secret places.
His fathers beheld, and they rejoiced and were glad;
Presents and gifts they brought unto him.
Then the lord rested, gazing upon her dead body,
While he divided the flesh of the ... , and devised a cunning plan.
He split her up like a flat fish into two halves;
One half of her he stablished as a covering for heaven.
He fixed a bolt, he stationed a watchman,
And bade them not to let her waters come forth.
He passed through the heavens, he surveyed the regions thereof,
And over against the Deep he set the dwelling of Nudimmud.
And the lord measured the structure of the Deep,
And he founded E-sara, a mansion like unto it.
The mansion E-sara which he created as heaven,
He caused Anu, Bel, and Ea in their districts to inhabit.

THE FIFTH TABLET

He (Marduk) made the stations for the great gods;
The stars, their images, as the stars of the Zodiac, he fixed.
He ordained the year and into sections he divided it;
For the twelve months he fixed three stars.
After he had ... the days of the year ... images,
He founded the station of Nibir [the planet Jupiter] to determine their bounds;
That none might err or go astray,
He set the station of Bel and Ea along with him.
He opened great gates on both sides,
He made strong the bolt on the left and on the right.
In the midst thereof he fixed the zenith;
The Moon-god he caused to shine forth, the night he entrusted to him.
He appointed him, a being of the night, to determine the days;
Every month without ceasing with the crown he covered him, saying:
"At the beginning of the month, when thou shinest upon the land,
Thou commandest the horns to determine six days,
And on the seventh day to divide the crown.
On the fourteenth day thou shalt stand opposite, the half....
When the Sun-god on the foundation of heaven...thee,
The ... thou shalt cause to ..., and thou shalt make his...
... unto the path of the Sun-god shalt thou cause to draw nigh,
And on the ... day thou shalt stand opposite, and the Sun-god shall...

... to traverse her way.
... thou shalt cause to draw nigh, and thou shalt judge the right.
... to destroy..."

[Nearly fifty lines are here lost.]

The gods, his fathers, beheld the net which he had made,
They beheld the bow and how its work was accomplished.
They praised the work which he had done...
Then Anu raised the ... in the assembly of the gods. He kissed the bow, saving, " It is...!"
And thus he named the names of the bow, saving,
"'Long-wood' shall be one name, and the second name shall be ...,
And its third name shall be the Bow-star, in heaven shall it...!"
Then he fixed a station for it...
Now after the fate of...
He set a throne...
...in heaven...
[The remainder of this tablet is missing.]

THE SIXTH TABLET

When Marduk heard the word of the gods,
His heart prompted him and he devised a cunning plan.
He opened his mouth and unto Ea he spake
That which he had conceived in his heart he imparted unto him:
"My blood will I take and bone will I fashion
I will make man, that man may
I will create man who shall inhabit the earth,
That the service of the gods may be established, and that their shrines may be built.
But I will alter the ways of the gods, and I will change their paths;
Together shall they be oppressed and unto evil shall they....
And Ea answered him and spake the word:
"... the ... of the gods I have changed
... and one...
... shall be destroyed and men will I...
... and the gods .
... and they..."

[The rest of the text is wanting with the exception of
the last few lines of the tablet, which read as follows.]

They rejoiced...
In Upsukkinnaku they set their dwelling.
Of the heroic son, their avenger, they cried:
" We, whom he succored.... !"

They seated themselves and in the assembly they named him...,
They all cried aloud, they exalted him...

THE SEVENTH TABLET

O Asari, [Marduk] "Bestower of planting," "Founder of sowing"
"Creator of grain and plants," "who caused the green herb to spring up!"
O Asaru-alim, [Mardk] "who is revered in the house of counsel," "who aboundeth in counsel,"
The gods paid homage, fear took hold upon them!

O Asaru-alim-nuna, [Marduk] "the mighty one," "the Light of the father who begat him,"
"Who directeth the decrees of Anu Bel, and Ea!"
He was their patron, be ordained their...;
He, whose provision is abundance, goeth forth...
Tutu [Marduk] is "He who created them anew";
Should their wants be pure, then are they satisfied;
Should he make an incantation, then are the gods appeased;
Should they attack him in anger, he withstandeth their onslaught!
Let him therefore be exalted, and in the assembly of the gods let him... ;
None among the gods can rival him!
15 Tutu [Marduk] is Zi-ukkina, "the Life of the host of the gods,"
Who established for the gods the bright heavens.
He set them on their way, and ordained their path;
Never shall his ... deeds be forgotten among men.
Tutu as Zi-azag thirdly they named, "the Bringer of Purification,"
"The God of the Favoring Breeze," "the Lord of Hearing and Mercy,"
"The Creator of Fulness and Abundance," " the Founder of Plenteousness,"
"Who increaseth all that is small."
In sore distress we felt his favoring breeze,"
Let them say, let them pay reverence, let them bow in humility before him!
Tutu as Aga-azag may mankind fourthly magnify!
"The Lord of the Pure Incantation," " the Quickener of the Dead,"
"Who had mercy upon the captive gods,"
"Who removed the yoke from upon the gods his enemies,"
"For their forgiveness did he create mankind,"
"The Merciful One, with whom it is to bestow life!"
May his deeds endure, may they never be forgotten ,
In the mouth of mankind whom his hands have made!
Tutu as Mu-azag, fifthly, his "Pure incantation" may their mouth proclaim,
Who through his Pure Incantation hath destroyed all the evil ones!"
Sag-zu, [Marduk] "who knoweth the heart of the gods," " who seeth through the innermost part!"
"The evil-doer he hath not caused to go forth with him!"
"Founder of the assembly of the gods," who ... their heart!"
"Subduer of the disobedient," "...!"

"Director of Righteousness," "...,"
" Who rebellion and...!"
Tutu as Zi-si, "the ...,"
"Who put an end to anger," "who...!"
Tutu as Suh-kur, thirdly, "the Destroyer of the foe,"
"Who put their plans to confusion,"
"Who destroyed all the wicked," "...,"
... let them... !

[There is a gap here of sixty lines. But somewhere among the lost lines belong the following fragments.]

who...
He named the four quarters of the world, mankind hecreated,
And upon him understanding...
"The mighty one...!"
Agil...
"The Creator of the earth...!"
Zulummu... .
"The Giver of counsel and of whatsoever...!"
Mummu, " the Creator of...!"
Mulil, the heavens...,
"Who for...!"
Giskul, let...,
"Who brought the gods to naught....!"
....
... " the Chief of all lords,"
... supreme is his might!
Lugal-durmah, "the King of the band of the gods," " the Lord of rulers."
"Who is exalted in a royal habitation,"
"Who among the gods is gloriously supreme!
Adu-nuna, " the Counselor of Ea," who created the gods his fathers,
Unto the path of whose majesty
No god can ever attain!
... in Dul-azag be made it known,
... pure is his dwelling!
... the... of those without understanding is Lugaldul-azaga!
... supreme is his might!
... their... in the midst of Tiamat,
... of the battle!

[Here follows the better-preserved ending.]

... the star, which shineth in the heavens.
May he hold the Beginning and the Future, may they pay homage unto him,
Saying, "He who forced his way through the midst of Tiamat without resting,

Let his name be Nibiru, 'the Seizer of the Midst'!
For the stars of heaven he upheld the paths,
He shepherded all the gods like sheep!
He conquered Tiamat, he troubled and ended her life,"
In the future of mankind, when the days grow old,
May this be heard without ceasing; may it hold sway forever!
Since he created the realm of heaven and fashioned the firm earth,
The Lord of the World," the father Bel hath called his name.
This title, which all the Spirits of Heaven proclaimed,
Did Ea hear, and his spirit was rejoiced, and he said:
"He whose name his fathers have made glorious,
Shall be even as I, his name shall be Ea!
The binding of all my decrees shall he control,
All my commands shall he make known! "
By the name of "Fifty " did the great gods
Proclaim his fifty names, they, made his path preeminent.

EPILOGUE

Let them [i.e. the names of Marduk] be held in remembrances and let the first man
proclaim them;
Let the wise and the understanding consider them together!
Let the father repeat them and teach them to his son;
Let them be in the ears of the pastor and the shepherd!
Let a man rejoice in Marduk, the Lord of the gods,
That be may cause his land to be fruitful, and that he himself may have prosperity!
His word standeth fast, his command is unaltered;
The utterance of his mouth hath no god ever annulled.
He gazed in his anger, he turned not his neck;
When he is wroth, no god can withstand his indignation.
Wide is his heart, broad is his compassion;
The sinner and evil-doer in his presence...
They received instruction, they spake before him,
... unto...
... of Marduk may the gods...;
... May they ... his name... !
... they took and...
.....................................!

END OF THE CREATION EPIC
THE FIGHT WITH TIAMAT

(ANOTHER VERSION)
**[Note: Strictly speaking, the text is not a creation-legend, though it gives a variant
form of the principal incident in the history of the creation according to the Enuma**

Elish. Here the fight with the dragon did not precede the creation of the world, but took place after men had been created and cities had been built.]

The cities sighed, men ...
Men uttered lamentation, they ...
For their lamentation there was none to help,
For their grief there was none to take them by the hand.
· Who was the dragon... ?
Tiamat was the dragon.....
Bel in heaven hath formed.....
Fifty kaspu [A kaspu is the space that can be covered in two hours travel, i.e. six or seven miles] in his length, one kaspu in his height,
Six cubits is his mouth, twelve cubits his...,
Twelve cubits is the circuit of his ears...;
For the space of sixty cubits he ... a bird;
In water nine cubits deep he draggeth...."
He raiseth his tail on high...;
All the gods of heaven...
In heaven the gods bowed themselves down before the Moon-god...;
The border of the Moon-god's robe they hastily grasped:
"Who will go and slay the dragon,"
And deliver the broad land from...
And become king over... ?
" Go, Tishu, slav the dragon,
And deliver the broad land from...,
And become king over...!"
Thou hast sent me, O Lord, to... the raging creatures of the river,
But I know not the... of the Dragon!

[The rest of the Obverse and the upper part of the Reverse of the tablet are wanting.]

REVERSE
....
And opened his mouth and spake unto the god...
" Stir up cloud, and storm and tempest!
The seal of thy life shalt thou set before thy face,
Thou shalt grasp it, and thou shalt slay the dragon."
He stirred up cloud, and storm and tempest,
He set the seal of his life before his face,
He grasped it, and he slew the dragon.
For three years and three months, one day and one night
The blood of the dragon flowed. ...

END OF

NECRONOMICON EX MORTIS

Lightning Source UK Ltd.
Milton Keynes UK
UKOW02n0053301116

288856UK00001B/1/P